About Ray Hawkins

Ray was born just before Christmas in 1938 at Rockdale, New South Wales to working class parents. After achieving the Intermediate School Certificate he worked as a lathe operator for a car engine repair firm then a labourer with his father's light steel fabrication business. He was sent to Sunday school at the local Church of Christ where he made his confession of faith and was baptized. At 21 years he was accepted as a student at the Churches of Christ Woolwich Bible College (Sydney). In 1963 Ray became the Student President of the College. That year he met his wife-to-be, Mary, who came to College for a two year missionary course. In 1964 they were married and over the years they became parents of three children.

Their major ministry emphasis has been in establishing two new Churches in NSW and preventing one from closure in Queensland. They also ministered in England. Ray has been NSW Conference President on two occasions, and NSW President for the Ministers' Association. He has been a Chaplain at the Green Hills Retirement village and Nursing Home (NSW). For 18 years he was involved with the Tenambit/Morpeth Rotary club becoming President and later made a 'Paul Harris Fellow'. Ray also became active with the 'Walk to Emmaus' movement and was Community Spiritual Director for Tasmania.

In his later years he went with Mary three times as part of short term mission trips to Africa. Out of that experience he wrote the 31 day devotional 'The Neurotic Rooster.' (It was a finance raiser for Eagles Wings in Zambia.) Now retired to Beauty Point, Tasmania, with Mary (who is a multi-published Inspirational Romance writer) he still preaches and is involved in establishing a Christian Fellowship there.

He is a regular contributor to 'The Upper Room' devotional magazine as well as having numerous articles, poems and studies from Scripture printed throughout his ministry. More information about Ray on www.mary-hawkins.com.

From Eden with Love
Published by Even Before Publishing;
a division of Wombat Books
P. O. Box 1519, Capalaba Qld 4157
www.evenbeforepublishing.com
www.wombatbooks.com.au

© Ray Hawkins 2011
Design and layout by Even Before Publishing

ISBN: 978-1-921633-41-6

National Library of Australia Cataloguing-in-Publication entry
Author: Hawkins, Raymond.
Title: From Eden with love/ Raymond Hawkins.
ISBN: 9781921633416 (pbk.)
Subjects: Marriage--Biblical teaching.
             Marriage--Religious aspects--Christianity.
             Love--Religious aspects--Christianity.
Dewey Number: 234.165

All rights reserved. No part of this publication may be reproduced, stored in, or introduced into a retreival system, or transmitted, in any form, or by any means (electronic, mechanical, photocopying, recording or otherwise) without the prior written permission of the publisher.

Unless otherwise indicated all Bible quotes are from the New International Version.

From Eden With Love

31 daily devotional meditations from the Bible concerning God's gift to a man and a woman

in life's most intimate

and

demanding relationship.

Dedication

To Mary who has helped me taste the promise of Eden

and

to understand the majesty and mystery of Marriage

Contents

About Ray Hawkins	1
The Symbolism of Marriage	7
The View from the Garden	9
The Noble Man Outlined	11
The Noble Woman	14
Marriage is being Yoked Together	16
The Art of Getting Along	19
Be Fruitful	21
The Husband's Crown	24
A Most Precious Jewel	26
Burden Bearers	29
Koinonia	32
Beware the Setting Sun	35
The Marriage Dance	37
Kisses Sweeter than Wine	39
A Sporting Affair	41
The Husband's Role Model	43
Role Model for Wife	45
The House Jesus Abides In	47
Love's Real Perfume (1)	49
Love's Real Perfume (2)	51
Recovering Love	53
Happy Ever After (1)	56
Happy Ever After (2)	58
There's an Art to Knowing	60
God's Centre for Marriage Renewal	62
The Highest Quality of Love	65
Keeping Marriage Holy	67
Cultivating Marriage	69
The Bride	71
The Bridegroom	73
The Marriage Supper	75
I'd Rather…	78

Day 1

The Symbolism of Marriage

Reading: Genesis 2:18-24.

Moses must have heard it wrong. Either that, or God was playing a trick on him. In the Genesis reading it says Adam gave 'birth', as it were, through 'surgery' to Eve. We know birth is the prerogative of the woman. Moses knew it also. Why then would he write it down and make it an integral part of Scripture?

The problem is compounded, if possible, by the Apostle Paul. "Man did not come from woman, but woman from man" (1 Corinthians 11:8). He stresses this again in 1 Timothy 2:13: "Adam was formed first, then Eve."

We know these men were not fools. They were not trying to be funny either. The Bible is a serious book promoting important issues with eternal consequences. Why then would this biologically impossible explanation of Adam giving birth, through surgery, to Eve be stated – twice?

Why? Because the Lord God was making a prophetic statement as well as a romantic one concerning marriage. He was also elevating and protecting the idea and the ideal which underpins the marriage. That is, marriage between a man and a woman. Because people do not believe, or understand, what Moses and Paul wrote, its meaning has been lost in the ease of living together without commitment and the leaving each other without regret.

The symbolism of marriage is designed by God, Father, Son, Holy Spirit, to point to something awesome. Adam represents Jesus who is called the second Adam (1 Corinthians 15:45). As the first Adam had his bride taken out of his side, so also when Jesus died on the cross and had His side pierced, His bride, the Church would emerge. The significance of this is also traced back to Eden. When Adam saw Eve he recognized the fact that she was bone of his bone and flesh of his flesh. In their sexual union they completed the God intended oneness once again. When the Lord Jesus gave birth to the Church its DNA is from Him. By faith we believe the Church is betrothed to the Creator and Lord. According to Revelation 19:7-8, there is a set day when all of Creation will witness a true marriage made in Heaven: "Let us rejoice and be glad and give him glory! For the wedding of the Lamb has come, and his bride has made herself ready! Fine linen, bright and clean, was given to her to wear." The Church's garment is said to represent the righteous acts of those who constitute the Church.

Herein dwells the mystery of marriage. Without it the only significance it has is according to the decrees of the country in which a couple 'tie the knot'. Unbelief and rejection of God's word robs the ceremony of its mystery. It has no foundation on which to exist. It has no future to which it points. It offers no sound reason for faithfulness within marriage, a problem with which converts out of paganism in Corinth had difficulty. Robbed of its spiritual significance there isn't any surprise in the way society has downgraded this beautiful ceremony (1 Corinthians 6:12-20).

For Christians Jesus is the supreme teacher and authority. What He says, goes! The religious leaders of His day tried to snare Him in a doctrinal issue about divorce. Jesus simply pointed them to the Genesis account. "Haven't you read, he replied, that at the beginning the Creator made them male and female, and said, for this reason a man will leave his father and mother and be united to his wife, and the two will become one flesh? So they are no longer two, but one" (Matthew 19:4-6).

In this statement Jesus adds another beautiful dimension to the significance of marriage. What was He referring to when He said the two become one? The account of God bringing Eve from out of the side of Adam and then becoming one again in the embrace of love! Within this framework can be found the reason why the Scriptures stress the importance of a Christian marrying a Christian. Every time this takes place there is a witness given to the World about what God did in the Garden, what will happen in the future, and the awesome implications of two becoming one.

In following devotions we will enjoy finding out some of the awe, some of the delights, some of the romance woven by God into the symbolism and testimony of marriage.

Reflect: When I think about Christ and the Church is there any symbolism reflected in my marriage, especially about the way I regard my 'other half?'

Prayer: Increase my appreciation and understanding of Christian marriage and give me opportunities to share this wonderful news to others, especially the young. Amen.

Day 2

The View from the Garden

Reading: Genesis 2:1-9, 21-22

More and more couples are holding their wedding service in gardens surrounded by the beauty of creation. It may be a sign of a loss of Christian values and understanding concerning marriage. It may also be an unconscious return to the original marriage service. For marriage was 'born' in a garden.

Prior to this event the Bible detailed the account of creation. The pinnacle of God's creative act was Adam. It becomes apparent as the Genesis story unfolds that the Lord God had a purpose in having Adam a solitary individual. Not only was the Lord presenting a theological insight for the future, but a lesson for Adam to take to heart. He had the world to himself but sensed something was missing, even in that perfect environment.

The Creator put the man into a deep sleep and from his 'rib' He brought into being the woman. Over the centuries a lot of humour and caustic remarks have arisen from this description of Eve's creation. The word 'rib' can also be translated as 'side'. Such an inference is much more meaningful that any twisted view stirred up by 'rib'. God was informing the man that the woman with whom he was to spend his life was his equal. They stood side by side and as such they were complete. Each had different, specific roles and accountabilities to God but one could not claim superiority over the other. The wedding 'service' in the Garden of Eden was a very simple and unique event. In fact the Lord God was not only the Celebrant He was also the best 'Man' and 'Father' of the bride. It was He who brought the woman to the man and bound them together with His love. From this event the later editor penned the words, "a man is to leave his parents and cleave only to his wife."

'Being married' isn't due to the service; it's in the becoming 'One flesh'. This beautiful and in many aspects mysterious term describes the intention of being married. It is becoming a whole person within the blessing of God where body, soul and spirit of the man are inter-linked with the body, soul and spirit of the woman. This explains the Bible's abhorrence for adultery and fornication (1 Corinthians 6:15, 16).

The number two within the Bible has special symbolism. It speaks of differences as one thing being different from another. It also points to how one can be of support to another. The strength of two witnesses to an event lies in the way their different understanding of what happened completes the overall picture. This symbolism is reflected within marriage. Each brings their differences which can be a danger for division or strength for mutual support. Becoming 'one flesh' is meant to be a witness to God's grace prevailing within the lives of the husband and wife.

How is this possible? The prayer of Jesus found in John 17 is about different groups of people finding unity in Christ Jesus. What the Lord Jesus prayed for His disciples has relevance for a married couple. He said, "Holy Father, protect them by the power of your Name...so that they may be one as we are one" (verse 11).

The closer a couple draw by faith to Jesus the more intimate they become with each other. This is due to both being on the same holy 'ground' and being mutually focused on their Lord and Saviour. The outcome of this is expressed by the writer of Ecclesiastes in 4:9-12: "Two are better than one, because they have a good return for their work: If one falls down his friend (read spouse) can help him up. But pity the man who falls and has no one to help him up! Also, if two lie down together, they will keep warm... Though one may be overpowered, two can defend themselves." The writer also adds, "A cord of three strands is not quickly broken." Surely within Biblical marriage that points to husband, wife and God.

Adam, in the sight of God, needed a 'helper'. Again this word has been seen as demeaning especially in our day and age. The trouble is people read back into the word their own dissatisfaction with their perceived meaning without appreciating the inherent dignity of the word. Psalm 33:20: "We wait in hope for the Lord; He is our help and shield." Psalm 146:5: "Blessed is he whose help is the God of Jacob, whose hope is in the Lord his God." If God is willing to be called a 'helper' why should any of us baulk at being called one?

Reflect: Marriage is God's idea. Am I looking at it from His or some one else's view?

Prayer: Thank you Almighty God for the eternal significance in being married. Thank you also for your resources offered to a man and woman to taste the joy of heaven by the people on earth. Amen.

Day 3

The Noble Man Outlined

Reading: 1 Timothy 3:1-10

A noble task requires a noble person. In God's Word He has defined both. Is He expecting perfection? Yes! Will it be forthcoming? No! However the Lord God continues to mould, shape, hone and polish the person to that end. In the reading it speaks of the noble task as being an Elder. To fulfil it God fashions the man.

In reviewing the qualifications, no surprise should be felt about how they would impact upon his wife and family. To lead the local expression of the Household of God, a man is expected to display similar leadership in the privacy of his home life. It is in the home scene where the armour suit of the shining knight in public has its rust spots uncovered. Many stories exist of disillusioned family members rejecting the Faith due to the husband/father being without his suit at home or not fixing the broken or rusted spots.

Every Christian man or boy should aspire to be Christ's noble man in private and public. Apart from the grace of God, the refining work of God's Word plus the perseverance of the noble man it will not happen. In the letter to Timothy are listed the various facets of the armour. Fortunate the wife whose husband seeks to be the noble knight dressed for the task.

Consider just a couple of the positive and negative features of the suit which helps define the man's inner being.

To be above reproach. Since conversion the man has grown in his faith, made restitution for his failures and has risen above the forces of false guilt and opposition. "But you, man of God...pursue righteousness, godliness, faith, love, endurance and gentleness...keep this command without spot or blame until the appearing of our Lord Jesus Christ" (1 Timothy 6:11-14).

To be able to teach. Teaching is more than eloquence from a platform or in a Bible School class. It embraces personal testimony backed up with lifestyle example. The motivation for living out what you believe is powerfully presented in Philippians 4:9: "Whatever you have learned or received or heard from me, or seen in me–put it into practice. And the God of peace will be with you."

Within the four walls of a nobleman's house is where the best teaching of God's grace and sustaining power comes to the fore. His lifestyle is providing a firm foundation on which his wife and children can firmly stand.

The spiritual suit of armour God has provided for the nobleman needs constant attention. Within society are forces designed to corrode, corrupt, and so cause him to stumble and fall. Within the human heart is also a selfish power which is irritated by God's righteous covering and the soul seeks to weaken God's grip over the life. Whenever the nobleman slips over and dirties his God–given clothing, he will never make excuses or seek to cover it over. Rather, he cries out in sorrow for forgiveness and the power to get up and walk again.

God is able to forgive the repentant, not the excuser of his actions.

Not given to drunkenness. This disease of a sin–sick soul has destroyed people, ministries and families. The nobleman must have alcohol in his power, not be under its control. God's call for abstinence was on the Nazarite or approved by Him on the Rechabite's oath. Otherwise God calls for self control.

"Do not get drunk on wine which leads to debauchery. Instead, be filled with the Spirit" (Ephesians 5:18). The former leads to violence and quarrels, the latter to health, holiness and happiness.

Not a lover of money. This is best answered from 1 Timothy 6:9,10. "People who want to get rich fall into temptation and a trap and into many foolish and harmful desires that plunge men into ruin and destruction. For the love of money is a root of all kinds of evil." The antidote is mentioned in verses 6-8: "Godliness with contentment is great gain. For we brought nothing into the world, and we can take nothing out of it. But if we have food and clothing, we will be content with that."

The husband who sets his heart on rising to this noble calling will be, and ever remain, the knight in shining armour to his wife and children.

Reflect: What would hinder me from being put on Christ's list of Noble men? What do I intend to do about getting it on, keeping it on?

Prayer: You are called the Potter, Heavenly Father. May I call you my Heavenly 'Blacksmith'? You and you alone can forge my armour. You and you alone can mend it when dented or rust affected. Lord, I want you to make me a nobleman in the eyes of my family. Amen.

Day 4

The Noble Woman

Reading: Proverbs 31:10-31

Reading the above reference could make the average woman feel rather inadequate. Being part of the sayings of King Lemuel, the passage indicates a lady living in a rather privileged position. Some fine issues mentioned however are applicable to women from less privileged strata's of society and should be taken note of. One such quote deals with the outward presentation, so easily faked, and the inner moral force of real attractiveness. "Charm is deceptive, and beauty is fleeting; but a woman who fears the Lord is to be praised" (verse 30). Why the praise? Because, "She speaks with wisdom and faithful instruction is on her tongue" (verse 26).

"She brings him (her husband) good, not harm, all the days of her life" (verse 12). Is this inferring she is a 'yes sir!' type of person? From the other descriptions of her personality and achievements this is highly unlikely. How could she do him good if he was embarking upon some venture in which she, not he, could see pitfalls and strife but remained silent? Any husband is unwise who fails to weigh the wisdom of his wife against the proposed venture and his understanding of the consequences. He must make the final decision. It must not be made in ignorance or from arrogance.

"She watches over the affairs of her household and does not eat the bread of idleness" (verse 27). In this man written book the majority of references to idleness are about men. Something has robbed such men of a sense of worth and made them indifferent to the welfare of their family. Lost also is their appreciation of accountability to their Creator and Redeemer. In the King James Version (KJV) laziness is often translated by sloth. If you have a picture in your mind of this tree lounging animal, you understand the implications. Ecclesiastes 10:18 puts it well: "If a man is lazy, the rafters sag; if his hands are idle, the house leaks." The noble wife will not allow the spirit of her home to sag or fail to address any leakage of faith and hope.

"She is clothed with strength and dignity" (verse 25). This woman has the resources and enterprise for business dealings and homecare. She delegates, initiates and in any company would be prominent. Not many women, single or married, have the opportunities assumed in this woman's life. The verse quoted above is available to all regardless of status in the eyes of a community. Because she fears the Lord, it allows Him to bless her with an inner strength, which wraps itself around her physical stature and enables her to fulfil her tasks with a positive attitude. She could very easily recite, "Surely God is my salvation; I will trust and not be afraid. The Lord, the Lord, is my strength and my song; he has become my salvation" (Isaiah 12:2).

"She can laugh at the days to come" (verse 25b). How would you understand the meaning behind this statement? Is it laughter stemming from confidence in her ability or from her fear of her Lord? Despite all her resources, ability and enthusiasm, life holds no guarantee such things will continue unchallenged or unchanged. Her laughter is an echo of the Messiah's laughter in Psalm two. Both are based upon the sovereign promises of Yahweh who is faithful to His promises. He and He alone is a person's security and hope, not materialism or position in life.

The question of verse 10, "A wife of noble character who can find" is answered in the verse which follows. "Many women do noble things" (verse29a) infers she was not the only one. Others could also be counted in the company. The verse goes on to say, "but you surpass them all." That's high praise.

Noble is applied to Ruth in the book named after her in chapter three and verse eleven. On the status gauge she would have been ranked quite low, however in God's eyes she was up there with this noble woman. This means that a woman from any social ranking has the capacity to be a noble woman if she set her heart and mind to it. The woman in Proverbs 31 isn't named. Maybe that is so any woman, from any background may aspire to be what Proverbs 12:4a points to: "A wife of noble character is her husband's crown."

Reflect: Am I my husband's crown? Would he evaluate my worth to him as more than rubies? Why?

Prayer: You have saved me and equipped me gracious Lord to be a noble woman. Help me to display it to my husband first and foremost, then to others I pray. Amen.

Day 5

Marriage is being Yoked Together

Reading: Malachi 2:13-16

In Philippians 4:3 the word 'yoke-fellow' is used by Paul. It's a fine expression for those involved in Christian marriage. Both are yoke-fellows. The idea of being 'yoked' means each will share equally the stress and strain of the load associated with living. It goes almost without saying that to be yoked requires both facing the same direction and learning the art of moving as one. A master craftsman would fashion a yoke to fit the particular team he was harnessing for the work. A poorly fitted or crafted yoke would create problems, distress, unnecessary hardships and damage to one or both of the team.

It's much easier to fashion a wooden yoke for animals than to have the spiritual equivalent applied to a man and woman entering into marriage. To enjoy this intimate relationship as God intended means we have to humble ourselves before the Master Craftsman and allow Him to fit our personalised yoke. If either one or the other partner continually resists the Master's measuring and fitting, no movement in the fulfilment of His purposes for 'the team of two' can get underway. The Lord Jesus requires a husband to actually lead the way in accepting the yoke. The wife must also be willing to put herself along side her husband. Neither should be too proud to wear the Lord's yoke. Matthew 11:28-30 can be applied to married couples as well as to individuals: "Come unto me, all you who are weary and burdened, and I will give you rest. Take my yoke upon you and learn from me, for I am gentle and humble in heart, and you will find rest for your souls. For my yoke is easy and my burden light."

If weariness begins to envelop a marriage it points to something not right in the mutual load sharing. When one is bearing the load alone sensing the other is malingering, resentment and irritability will creep in. If the Master was managing animals He could simply step in and deal with the animal's problem. Because He has given us the right of choice and co-operation, the Master of fulfilled marriages must wait for our permission. Notice the above 'to come to Him' is an invitation to the person, and the couple, with the expectation of a reply. This allows for the possibility of either acceptance or rejection. Many a Christian marriage has fallen down right there as unwillingness to bow before the Lord creates a self destructing stubbornness. In the reading from Malachi the prophet highlights the consequences of such hardness of the heart. In chapter 2:14 the words "you have broken faith" are used. For whatever reason the yoke of the covenant of marriage had been put off, shattered, Yahweh wasn't happy.

What Malachi wrote on behalf of the Lord remains true today Why was the Lord so antagonistic towards the breaking of the bonds between a husband and wife? It has to do with the concept of being 'one'. Jesus quotes this in Matthew 19:3-12 and uses the word relating to marriage as being 'yoked together' in verse 6 where it is translated as 'joined together'. When two leave the 'yoke relationship' physically, emotionally or spiritually, there is a wound inflicted upon the holy purpose of God embodied in marriage. There is also a wound upon each soul which needs attention and healing.

In Matthew 5:32 our Lord didn't rule out the possibility of divorce due to marital unfaithfulness. Such an event isn't something which pleases Him. In fact, divorce is a testimony that one or the other in the marriage isn't walking in obedience to the Lord and His Word. For in 1John 1:7 it clearly states, "if we walk in the light as He is in the light, we have fellowship with one another and the blood of Jesus, His Son, purifies us from all sin." This doesn't imply that God doesn't love those in the 'broken yoke' club. He loves them eternally. He is however sad for them and the hurt they have endured unnecessarily.

When worn under the supervision of the Master, the wonder of the yoke is appreciated more and more as the years pass. Initially our individual natures find it uncomfortable to adjust to another and at the same time understand and heed the voice of the Lord. However as we obey by faith and trust, the discovery is made we don't want to be without our 'yoke-fellow'. God has woven two hearts into one, blessed each to be a blessing to the other. The 'yoke' has become a 'badge' of beauty and unity under the Master's hand.

Reflect: How well is the 'yoke' sitting on my heart at this moment? Do I need to go and have a talk with the Master about some burr that's got under it or something that needs adjusting?

Prayer: I praise your Name, Lord Jesus, for the person you have given to me. Thank you that we are yoke-fellows on the journey of life. For your patience to us as well as your skilful 'harnessing' of body, soul and spirit, I bow in awe before you. Amen.

Day 6
The Art of Getting Along

Reading: Psalm 25:1-15

Strike a match and the resulting friction produces fire. The flame can be used to warm the house or burn it down, depending on the person's intent. Friction within a relationship can have similar emotional results. In marriage so much depends upon the character of the couple when they clash over something. Can they rise above the friction and the verbal sparks produced? Is it the beginning of a crack within the relationship or a learning experience to bind them closer together? Will the husband and wife express prudence (careful thought in acting and planning) or folly as they seek to press their point of view? These two opposing forces appear time and again in the book of Proverbs and the results of each are listed.

No one is born with the companionship of Prudence. This beautiful Governor of relationships makes herself know through life's experiences. However, she is only recognisable to the teachable. How important then it is for the couple to want to learn to understand each other. From that desire they will come to grips with the realities of married life and at the same time enjoy each other's differences. God has not left us ignorant of how to get along together and foil folly. His Word is a great relationship manual. In it you can meet Prudence and friends. One friend is known as Wisdom. Prudence is able to bring this friend to the fore in situations where tensions have arisen. Wisdom is such a wonderful and gracious companion to be associated with in marriage. Her capacity to soothe hurting minds and ease burdened hearts shouldn't be underestimated.

God has a climbing map for those wanting to experience the heights to which their wedding day pointed. What the Lord will not do is read it for the climbing duo. The cry of their hearts must go up, "Teach me the way I should go. Give me the wisdom to walk it. Strengthen me to persevere." The writer of the 119th psalm must have uttered something similar. He recorded his understanding of the answer: "Your word is a lamp unto my feet and a light unto my path" (Ps. 119:105).

Regardless of how much in love a husband and wife continue to be, disagreements arise during the climb. Left unattended, the sparks generated will cause the fires of resentment, indifference plus an unreasoning hardness of heart. Within the marital relationship especially there is need for Prudence's calming role. God has ordained that this elegant attitude assist the husband and wife in understanding, accepting and respecting each other in areas of friction. "Your statutes are wonderful; therefore I obey them. The unfolding of your words gives light; it gives understanding to the simple" (Psalm 119:129-130).

Prudence never works alone. You meet her companions in Proverbs 8:12. You know about Wisdom, now meet Knowledge and Understanding. Together they form the fabulous four attitudes essential for climbing to the heights of the marriage mountain. On the way they help the linked duo to recognize God's provisions by which He nourishes their lives to enjoy, and be strengthened for the climb.

Allowing Prudence to be the Governor of relationships requires a meek and righteous heart with God. It would be wrong to think she could not be offended or cowered by her host. This is always the emotional and spiritual struggle a Christian has within himself or in the bonds of holy matrimony. Self-righteousness so easily asserts itself and desires to rule. This unholy attitude also has companions called Intolerance and Covetousness. The Holy Spirit challenges this destructive trio with the victory of the Cross. Subduing them is only possible when the host in which they romp repents, confesses he has erred and seeks cleansing through the poured out life of Jesus Christ at Calvary.

Prudence would point a person, or a couple, to David's wonderful 139th Psalm. This is a pre-emptive strike against the terrible trio of Self-righteousness, Intolerance and Covetousness: "Search me, O God, and know my heart; test me and know my anxious thoughts. See if there is any offensive way in me, and lead me in the way everlasting" (Psalm 139:23-24).

Now *that is* being prudent!

Reflect: How teachable am I? What have I learnt lately to make my mountain climb an exciting time? How have I assisted the one, to whom I'm linked, appreciate the climb?

Prayer: Lord, I would like the Fabulous Four Attitudes to be strong in my heart and mind. As I learn your word and apply it to my life, I do hope they will grow strong in me and cause me to glorify your Name. Amen.

Day 7
Be Fruitful

Reading: John 15:1-17

The first recorded commission is found in Genesis 1:28: "God blessed them and said to them, 'Be fruitful and increase in number, fill the whole earth and subdue it'." Today we can say the descendents of Adam and Eve have certainly increased. However, what about being fruitful?

To simply apply the commission to bearing and raising children is to miss the far deeper implications. This is especially true in the lives of couples who desire children but for reasons beyond their control cannot conceive. 'Increase in number' means what it says, however how can we understand the being fruitful part? As the Scriptures reveal, being fruitful has personal application to a quality of life and relationships. Within marriage, God has a special interest in wanting a couple to know and enjoy this quality of life.

In our reading you noticed that God the Father is called the Gardener. He is both a wine grape grower and orchardist of the spirit. He desires fruit from His children. It is by our fruitfulness men and women outside His kingdom are made aware of God's tender skills. Colossians 1:10 says, "... we pray this in order that you may live a life worthy of the Lord and may please Him in everyway: bearing fruit in every good work, growing in the knowledge of God..." What is called for in a person's life is also called for by our Lord in the lives of a married couple.

The 'fruit' of a person's life brings glory to God but in essence it isn't for Him. Nor is it for the 'tree'. Fruit is for others to enjoy. Within the marital environment such fruit is meant to be of the highest quality and very delicious for the other to enjoy. Behind the passage in Galatians 5:22-23 concerning the Fruit of the Spirit is the recognition of it being consumed by others. Think of the times your spouse needed the fruit of love mixed with joy because of some outside pressures siphoning off her/his energy. Was it found in you? Think of the nutritious power of peace and patience to an anxious partner. Consider the emotional and renewing vitamins in the fruit of kindness, goodness and faithfulness. When your spouse can feed on your gentleness and self-control how satisfying your fruitfulness will be in her/his life. "What about me?" you may well exclaim. Your husband or wife should also be cultivating, under the Gardener's direction, similar fruit for you.

There is a tendency to believe we can produce such fruit by our own efforts and desires. Impossible! For this is a spiritual dimension and must be planted within our inner being by the grace and goodness of God. The prophet Hosea grasped this in relation to his nation, Israel, when he quoted Yahweh as saying, "…your fruitfulness comes from me" (Hosea 14:8).

Within every life and relationship unwanted and distressing circumstances intrude. We can react to them with bitterness and unbelief, which will blight our personal life. Also our marital fruitfulness would be frost bitten or hail damaged. This isn't God's intention for us. May we prepare our hearts, relationship and marriage testimony from reading and applying principles from the life of Joseph recorded in Genesis. Betrayed by jealous brothers and sold into captivity, he was unjustly accused of impropriety and condemned to a foul Egyptian jail. How tempted he must have been to doubt his God's favour and promises. Joseph however clung to them when it all seemed so pointless. Later, through God's overruling he was taken out of prison and placed in a governing position. Joseph married and had two sons, Ephraim and Manasseh. After the birth of Manasseh, Joseph cried, "God has made me fruitful in the land of my suffering" (Genesis 41:52). Regardless of circumstances, God is able to make your life, relationship and marriage fruitful. This requires you to trust Him, wait on His overruling and continue to apply God's spiritual and emotional nutrients.

There can be an unnecessary sadness develop as the senior years roll over a married couple. A sense of outliving usefulness and of simply marking time can give our fruitfulness a touch of 'frost-bite'. Even in our old age the Lord has provided for us to be fruitful so family, friends and onlookers can pluck from our testimony fruit that offers hope in time and eternity. Psalm 92:12-14 sums it up nicely: "The righteous will flourish like the palm tree…they will still bear fruit in old age, they will stay fresh and green."

Reflect: Blessed is the man and woman whose delight is in the law of the Lord, and on His law they meditate day and night. They are like a tree planted by the streams of water, which yields its fruit in season and whose leaf does not wither (adapted from Psalm 1:2-3).

Prayer: O God my Father, Gardener of my heart and marriage may I yield my will to you, and trust in your skill to produce the fruit of your choice in me for the needs of my spouse. May I live under the guidance and government of your Spirit and be nurtured by your Word I pray. Amen.

Day 8

The Husband's Crown

Reading: Proverbs 5:15-19

I'm a commoner! There's no hint of royalty or aristocracy in my heritage. In fact being an Australian there is more, much more, likelihood of my genes carrying convict history. Still I can honestly say, "I've a crown I wear with pride." You see, according to Proverbs 12:4 my wife is my crown: "A wife of noble character is her husband's crown." The Hebrew word for crown refers to either a royal or bridal crown. On my wedding day I wore the 'bridal crown'. Now, in my everyday experiences, I enjoy the 'royal crown'.

The book of Proverbs is a nitty-gritty collection of quotes saturated with sayings from experiences and relationships. It is a must read for all ages. Consider the passage set for the daily reading: A smile might have come across your face as your read some of the expressions and metaphors about the wife. The meaning, however, is inescapable. There are forces within any society to weaken and break a marriage and in the early chapters of Proverbs one is confronted head on. In chapter 5 the writer provides an antidote against being 'bitten'. He also supplies spectacles to guard against being hypnotised by another's charm. The antidote and the spectacles point to an ongoing, unrelenting and maturing fascination and commitment by a husband to loving his wife.

Within the intimacy of marriage a thirst best described as passion develops due to the interaction of two personalities. The heart longs for this thirst to be satisfied. In 1 Corinthians 7:3-5 wise words on marital intimacy are recorded: "The husband should fulfil his marital duty to his wife and likewise the wife to her husband. The wife's body does not belong to her alone but also to her husband. In the same way, the husband's body does not belong to him alone but also to his wife. Do not deprive each other except by mutual consent and for a time, so that you may devote yourselves to prayer: Then come together again so that Satan will not tempt you because of your lack of self control."

The writer of Proverbs is majoring on the husband's attitude to and emotional estimation of the wife. He depicted her as a 'fountain'. Fountains are a work of art, pleasing to the eye and refreshing to the soul. The man has a responsibility to bless his 'fountain' and to rejoice in her. This requires wisdom, as well as understanding of her needs, strengths and weaknesses. In a beautiful love book called The Song of Songs (NIV translation of Song of Solomon), the writer there describes the wife also as a beautiful fountain: "you are a garden fountain, a well of flowing water streaming down from Lebanon" (4:15). As the years roll over a married couple, the 'fountain' should become more beautiful and satisfying because the husband has cared for her with loving kindness and attention.

Rejoicing as a husband with and about your wife resonates with the sound of enjoying a party. There is no better way for a man and woman to enjoy the beauty and intimacy of being one flesh than to love, honour, and obey each other. The words of Ecclesiastes 9:9a endorse this when it says, "enjoy life with your wife, whom you love, all the days of this meaningless life that God has given you under the sun." The writer of that book was having a tough time as he wrestled with the issues of life and yet he knew that in the embrace of his wife, he as a husband found meaning and joy. In Deuteronomy 24:5 a recently married man is instructed to rejoice in his new wife. How can this happen? By making her his priority! This would come through the commitment to love, to esteem her as the gift of God and to enjoy her favours as well as bestowing his upon her.

For the wife to remain the husband's crown requires him to be captivated by her love. The crown radiates the glory of the marriage when the man is spellbound by the woman at his side. The NKJV translation of the Song of Songs expresses this spell: "You have ravished my heart, my sister, my spouse; you have ravished my heart with one look of your eyes, with one link of your necklace. How fair is your love, my sister, my spouse! How much better than wine is your love, and the scent of your perfumes than all spices! Your lips, O my spouse, drip as the honeycomb; honey and milk are under your tongue" (4:9-11).

Reflect: How well am I displaying my joy in 'wearing' my crown in the home and on the street? Am I captivated by my fountain and dedicated to her well-being? If I'm the wife and crown, how do I radiate my pleasure? When considered as the fountain, how refreshing am I to him?

Prayer: I'm in debt to you, Almighty God, for many things but there is one special gift of gratitude I must express. For the woman you have given me to stand by my side, to help bear the load, may I cherish her and satisfy the needs of her heart too. Amen.

Day 9

A Most Precious Jewel

Reading: Matthew 19:1-6

God gave Adam and Eve a most precious jewel when He brought them together in marriage. This gem could not be the possession of one without the other otherwise it would be tarnished. The Judeo-Christian concept of marriage derived from Genesis is a priceless gift from Heaven to the future inhabitants of earth as a trust from the Almighty God.

The wayward heart of humankind with its arrogance has despised this gift and twisted it to suit the sinful and self-indulgent, soul nature. The World system has fashioned a nasty, disposable, caricature of what God created and the result has had devastating effects upon children, society and the most intimate relationship designed by the Lord.

In His mercy the Lord never took back His jewel. Within the vault of His Scriptures it still can be found by people of faith in Christ. This precious gem sparkles within marriage due to the commitment each has to the other. In Hebrews 13:4 we read, "Marriage should be honoured by all, and the marriage bed kept pure." The Greek word used for 'honoured' signifies something precious and costly. Again, it is a jewel, which can only be worn by two under the umbrella of God's grace. Imagine in another context receiving a wonderful diamond necklace. What effect would it have upon you? There would be a change in your attitude and behaviour as you would prize it, guard it and display it. However, your wearing of it doesn't add anything to the value or beauty of the diamond necklace, rather, it enhances your bearing. In a similar fashion that is what God had in mind when He gave Adam and Eve, and their descendants, the gem of marriage.

The priceless gift is not a matter of outward appearance, performance or status. It can only be worn in the heart and displayed within the unity of the one flesh principle of marriage. When worn according to Heaven's instructions, this mutual jewel of the heart increases in value and beauty as the years come and go.

We have become so conditioned by the caricature of marriage and the cheapening of it by 'plastic' imitations there's a need to re-evaluate it. This can be done by a comparison of the Greek word for honoured in other contexts. Within the translations of the New Testament the word is presented as 'precious' or 'costly stones'.

"…you were redeemed from the empty way of life handed down to you from your forefathers… (by) the *precious* blood of Christ" (1 Peter 1:18, 19).

"…(God) has given us His very great and *precious* promises, so that through them you may participate in the divine nature and escape the corruption in the world caused by evil desires" (2 Peter 1:4).

The apostle Paul reminded the Corinthians that sometime in the future their Christian life and work will be tested. This Judgement will be by God Himself through the fire of His presence. Paul says to them and to us not to build a life of straw nor let our service be as sticks which will burn. What is needed is to construct on the spiritual foundation of faith in Jesus Christ "gold, silver, *costly stones*…" 1 Corinthians 3:12. This covers every aspect of our lives. Can you begin to grasp how the Bible upholds the integrity and awesome extravagance God has invested in faith based, grace under-pinned, God ordained marriage?

Into the hands of His trusted men and women united in marriage the Lord God has placed the continuing honour of marriage. This heavenly gem is kept radiant and safe by their marriage bed remaining pure. That purity is a reflection of the purity and passion of glory. Peter uses the word for pure in 1 Peter 1:3, 4: "Praise be to the God and Father of our Lord Jesus Christ (who)… has given us new birth…into an inheritance that can never perish, spoil or fade…" The words 'can never spoil' is the same word translated in Hebrews 13:4 as 'pure' and in the KJV as 'undefiled'. God has entrusted a magnificent jewel to men and women. It is their responsibility, under God, to prevent it being defiled.

Unfortunately, disciples of Christ can be influenced by the values of the World and treat lightly what God highly esteems. The words of Paul to the Romans have special relevance to any contemplating marriage or who have entered into this sacred institution. "I urge you, brothers, in view of God's mercy, to offer your bodies as living sacrifices, holy, and pleasing to God – this is your spiritual act of worship. Do not be conformed any longer to the pattern of this world, but be transformed by the renewing of your mind" (Romans 12:1-2).

To look at your marriage through God's eyes will transform you both and protect your relationship from the World's defiling counterfeits.

Reflect: How proudly are we displaying the 'jewel' of Heaven in our marital relationship?

Prayer: Forgive us Lord if we have allowed the 'dust of neglect' to collect on the precious gem you gave us when we united our lives in marriage. May we take a new, deeper insight into our relationship and by your grace make this gem sparkle again. Amen.

Day 10
Burden Bearers

Reading: Ephesians 3:16-4:3

Going to the gym is proving a very popular means of improving health and gaining fitness. In my growing years I didn't see the need for such a program as I was involved in the construction business and was used to heavy weights and plenty of walking. However there was one type of gymnasium I would have benefited from in the lead up to getting married. I don't imagine such a gym exists but it certainly would be beneficial to men (and women) if they are similar to me.

The program I needed would have been to build up my emotional, intellectual and spiritual stamina for being a husband. I'm sure my wife would have agreed. She recognises how she could have benefited from a similar course.

When anyone sees another struggling under a load it is easy to go and offer to help carry it, even for a short distance. What happens when the burden is invisible to the naked eye? No offers of help are forthcoming and yet such unseen burdens are often more grievous to bear and harmful to the soul. Unfortunately within the marriage union one or both partners can suffer from this insensitivity and blindness to the weight on the other's heart.

Fortunately, those who pick up a Christian Bible discover it is a wonderful manual for personal inner development and sensitivity training. More than that, it also offers a personal trainer to assist in this gymnasium of spirit and soul. The passage quoted at the beginning encouraged the Ephesian believers to walk worthy of their calling. This can be applied to general situations and most definitely to the marriage union. The practical outcome of this endeavour is to equip both partners for the most intensive journey of relational and self discovery ever designed. It is called Christian marriage.

Ephesians 3:16 outlines the purpose of the 'work-out': "I pray that out of his glorious riches he may strengthen you with power through his Spirit in your inner being." It takes the grace and power of the Lord Jesus to draw you into the fitness regime and His importance in your life to keep at it.

Jesus lays the foundation for what is to come in an understanding of true love. When you are "rooted and established in love" you will have power to grasp and know the "love which surpasses knowledge". Without this foundation the demands of being a burden bearer in Christian marriage will either crack under the strain or suffer spiritual 'rotting'.

Ephesians 4:1 as applied to the Christian couple's calling lets us know in no uncertain terms we are to live worthy lives. This will be reflected in our calling as believers together in Christ. As you read on you come across words which the soul finds unpleasant. Here is where the manual and our personal trainer begin to apply the pressure to develop inner strength. To choose the soft option is to remain emotionally and spiritually flabby.

Ephesians 4:2 confronts us with four ongoing disciplines to master. Each one affects different facets of our inner life and outlook with a direct impact upon being sensitive to how the 'other half' is travelling.

The first one is *humility* - easy to quote hard to define. The best illustration comes from Jesus in the upper room. He washed and wiped the disciples' feet. He urged His followers to adopt a similar attitude. Taking the 'basin and towel' principle reveals the strength of knowing who you are and being willing to put others before self-interest. The Lord's example and training can prevent a lot of unnecessary friction between spouses if practised.

Gentleness follows on from humility. How precious is this attitude and so necessary when the one loved is fragile. What Jesus applied to Himself in Matthew 11:28-30 has a lovely application to a married couple. Gentleness is inner 'muscle' deliberately yoked to the weakness of the other so as to empower him/her to handle the burden of the moment. In marriage there will be times when the husband will be in need and the inner resources of the wife will be yoked to him. There will be times when the role needs will be reversed and the husband will ease the strain.

Within marriage there are moments when we irritate each other, hopefully not at the same time. Such matters need to be understood and remedied but at the right time and after prayerful preparation. Under these conditions you need the stamina to be *patient* or as the KJV puts it, *'long-suffering'*. What this achieves is a desire not to react but to understand, then at the right moment to resolve it. When we understand that the Lord is patient to us in our salvation and every day affairs we will want to express the same attitude to our loved one.

All of this brings us to *'bearing with each other in love.'* Love initiates it and completes it. However we have to bear with each other and that is only possible as love is exercised in *humility, gentleness and patience*. It's only when we follow the manual and obey the Life Trainer will these qualities grow strong within us to prevail over our self-centeredness and self-righteousness.

Reflect: Carry each other's burdens, and in this way you will fulfil the law of Christ" (Galatians 6:2). How can this be put into practice in your marital relationship?

Prayer: Lord there are times, perhaps many times when I want to skip going to the 'gym'. I get weary, and self-centeredness sneaks in and my spiritual life gets flabby. I'm so glad you are patient with me and through various means stir up the desire to gain inner strength again. I want to be strong so as to be ready at any time to be a burden bearer for my wife (husband) as she (he) has been a burden bearer for me. Amen.

Day 11

Koinonia

Reading: 1 John 1:1-9

In the New Testament the Greek word koinonia is translated by such English words as 'Communication, Communion, Contribution, Distribution, Fellowship.' Have a re-read of those words and place them in the context of your marriage. It doesn't take long to realise how important such a word as 'koinonia' is for a husband and wife, and indeed for any children within their embrace. Below are some passages where 'koinonia' is variously translated and you can reflect upon them as they have bearing upon you and your spouse (The English word is highlighted.)

"God, who has called you into *fellowship* with His Son Jesus Christ our Lord, is faithful" (1 Corinthians 1:9). As husband and wife you will know a growing and deepening relationship as you both respond to the call of the Father. Part of it is to know Him in and through obedient faith in Jesus as Lord. The passage set for reading stresses the principle concerning the spiritual dimensions for mutual fellowship. 'Koinonia' depends upon walking in the Light, a metaphor for being in harmony with the teaching and character of Jesus Christ. How do we measure this? Simple! It's by how we treat each other. John uses illustrations about hating, neglecting, showing no pity to fellow Christians. James says similar things in his letter. Applying this to marriage we cannot have fellowship with the Lord if, as husbands, we be-little our wives; neither can we have fellowship with the Lord if, as wives, we neglect the husband's welfare; there is no way either can say they enjoy the good things of God if they persist in doing what is offensive to Him. When broken, fellowship as desired by God is only restored by repentance, restitution and renewal.

"As for Titus, he is my *partner* and fellow-worker among you" (2 Corinthians 8:23). Paul expressed to the Corinthians that his ministry was a partnership venture, and he mentioned Titus especially in this passage. Here again is a wonderful application for understanding 'koinonia' in marriage. It is a partnership. The wife and husband are companions, fellow-workers under the Lord and as such should seek to honour Him before the gaze of friend and foe. When one forgets marriage is a partnership and treats the other as an inferior, there can be no Biblical appreciation or enjoyment of 'koinonia'.

"Because of the service by which you have proved yourselves, men will praise God for the obedience that accompanies your confession of the Gospel of Christ, and for your generosity *in sharing with* them and with everyone else" (2 Corinthians 9:13). One of the amazing things we discover about the Lord Jesus over time is His grace and generosity. He has blessed us with every spiritual blessing according to Ephesians 1:3. What our Lord has done for us motivates us to do for others. Generosity of spirit and resources is an expression of 'koinonia'. Within the walls of the family home this spiritual dimension of grace should abound. We cannot walk with the Lord, enjoy His bounty and be a scrooge to our beloved.

"I pray that you may be active in *sharing* your faith, so that you will have a full understanding of every good thing we have in Christ" (Philemon 6). In this verse what is being shared is the Faith. Often one or both partners may find it difficult in the early stages of marriage to freely share about their Faith journey. This could be due to personality, upbringing, a sense of ignorance or unworthiness and even a fear of being put down. There is however nothing which can compare to the times when a man and woman share the good things of God. When the going gets tough either personally, at work, in health or the family scene, there is a certain strength, comfort and joy in being able to share it with the person joined in holy wedlock! Flowing out of this 'koinonia' is a therapeutic and tender atmosphere felt by all. It may take time for a husband or wife to be encouraged to this depth of relationship but the blessing enjoyed is worth the effort and time involved.

"May the grace of the Lord Jesus Christ, and the love of God, and the *fellowship* of the Holy Spirit be with you all" (2 Corinthians 13:26). Such a lovely benediction by Paul to the Corinthian Church! Surely the Lord wants marriages to live under the same benediction. In the KJV, *fellowship* becomes *communion*. I rather like that word in this context for it has the aroma of worship in it. May you and your beloved enjoy together all the aspects within the Greek word 'koinonia', and together make your marriage an expression of worship and celebration.

Reflect: What aspects of 'koinonia' are strong within my marriage and what areas may need some attention?

Prayer: Lord Jesus, as the Light of the World, shine strongly in our world. May your word be a light upon our walk together and direct our hearts and minds to enjoy your 'koinonia' together. Amen.

Day 12
Beware the Setting Sun

Reading: Ephesians 4: 25-32

A 33 year old man in India had an argument with his wife. He stormed out of the house and climbed up a tree. For the next 50 years that was where he lived. His stubborn and unforgiving heart prevented him from attending his son's wedding and also his grand-daughter's wedding (The Australian newspaper, May 8th, 2006).

In the light of the above, Ephesians 4:26 becomes wise counsel for any relationship: "In your anger do not sin: Do not let the sun go down while you are still angry, and do not give the Devil a foothold."

There are four words exposing various shades of anger in Ephesians 4. In verse 26 are two and verse 31 another two. They are used deliberately and skilfully to warn the readers of the calamity this natural passion can reap when used by our sinful nature. In the intense relationship of marriage such a passion has the power to destroy intimacy and crush initiatives.

The anger you don't want the sun to set upon refers to a strong emotional disposition burning with resentment and seeking revenge. In the Upper Hunter Valley of New South Wales is a place called 'Burning Mountain'. Sometime in the distant past the coal beneath the surface caught fire and it has never been extinguished. In spiritual terminology that is what Paul is warning about. The tragedy of this condition is seen year in and year out in wrecked lives and scorched families.

All anger does not stem from sin. If a person cannot get angry over injustice and exploitation there is deadness in his spirit. Jesus was angry when He overturned the tables of the Temple money changers. It was anger on behalf of His Heavenly Father, not about how they treated Jesus. However, most anger within relationships arises from feeling injured, taken advantage of or not getting one's own way. Left to fester in the heart, this sinful attitude will erupt through word, deed or sullen attitude. Healing of the soul must precede reaching out with forgiveness to the one who has caused offence and wounded the heart. To be honest before the Lord God about how you feel allows Him to anoint your heart with His grace. He then empowers you in the words of Ephesians 4:32: "Be kind and compassionate to one another, forgiving each other, just as in Christ God forgave you."

The Lord Jesus calls His disciples to a higher life, a more vigorous self-control and a more honest accounting of our inner being. In Ephesians 4 is the illustration of taking off and putting on emotional and spiritual clothes. Instead of excusing ourselves we are instructed to exercise our commitment and will-power to allow the Holy Spirit to dress us in true righteousness and holiness.

We all want to be heroes in the eyes of our loved ones. The Bible encourages us to be just that, not in the military or sporting sense but in the relational. "Better a patient man than a warrior, a man who controls his temper than one who takes a city" (Proverbs 16:32). If there were more husbands who were considered heroes by their wives and children, there would be less domestic violence and delinquency. "He who guards his mouth and his tongue keeps himself from calamity" (Proverbs 21:23). How wonderful it is when the wife applies herself, in the same manner, to be a heroine to her husband and children.

To live your life by the principle of the setting sun can be humbling. At the same time it is very liberating. It's also good for personal health and the rewards go beyond hugs and kisses. The Devil becomes a loser in his endeavours to spoil the work of the Holy Spirit within the marriage of Christians because he cannot keep the anger seething throughout the night.

When Christ controls a marriage there is no fear of the setting sun.

Reflect: "…patience is better than pride. Do not be quickly provoked in your spirit, for anger resides in the lap of fools" (Ecclesiastes 7:8b, 9).

Prayer: Oh Lord, I want to be a hero to my wife, not a fool. You know how hard this is for me. As I bow before you I cry for strength to put off my 'old nature' and put on that which is pleasing in your sight. I'm so glad nothing is too hard for you to do. Praise be to your Name. Amen.

Day 13

The Marriage Dance

Reading: Jeremiah 31:1-14

I remember as a teenager plucking up the courage to go and learn to dance. At first it felt awkward. I was nervous, reticent and clumsy. My teacher endured many a sore toe and scrapped shin before I became reasonably proficient in a variety of dances.

When I married I began to realise I was in an unending dance. Both of us were beginners. Some good coaches on the 'sidelines' encouraged us. It was up to us, however, to learn the steps and sense the rhythm of the marriage dance. More than sore toes and scrapped shins resulted from our practicing the required steps. Egos felt bruised as emotions rose from being stepped upon. Combine all that with uncertainty or disagreement about what tune we were dancing to, you realise the marriage dance can lead one or the other to sit it out. Perhaps one of the hardest things was to hear the same melody and sway to the same beat. It's easy to embrace in the marriage dance. It's another thing to maintain the embrace when life offers an orchestra with unfamiliar, conflicting or unwanted music.

Words used for dancing in the Old Testament include 'turn around', twist (long before Rock and Roll made it fashionable!) and to skip. It seems as though this gives us all scope to dance before the Lord and do it in step with our partner. Psalm 150:4 encourages us to "praise him with tambourine and dancing, praise him with the strings and flute."

God intended marriage to be on the 'dance floor' of everyday living. Husbands and wives were to feel the rhythm of God's music in the midst of earth's cacophony. They were meant to know that the skill in marriage comes though faithfulness and persistence in understanding and appreciating each other. The more times you dance together, the closer you grow together. The closer you are the sweeter the dance. The sweeter the dance the more varied the steps. The more varied the steps the more exhilarating the embrace. The more exhilarating the embrace, the more wonderful the dance! For that to be true, God must be the dance Master as well as the orchestra Leader.

Dancing, as with any other aspect of life, can be a blessing or a curse. In Scripture when it is associated with idolatry, dancing destroys morality and relationships. Performed in righteousness and under the gaze of God, dancing was an expression of victory and joy. (Exodus 15:20, 21, Jeremiah 31:13.) The spiritual significance of those verses finds expression within the marriage dance. Surely there are moments when your heart leaps for joy and your feet want to follow. How precious to hold your husband or wife in a warm embrace and celebrate together.

One such occasion could easily be found in Luke 15 and the story of the prodigal son. When he returned home a celebration was held. As the Lord tells the story, this was a time for feasting, music and dancing. How wonderful! The word there for music means symphony. How appropriate! When a broken relationship is healed the symphony of grace is the music played in the house of the redeemed.

Another great occasion for the marriage dance is recorded in Psalm 30. Within this psalm David pours out his heart to God in testimony and praise. His words can find many echoes in the dramas married couples (and of course, singles) share in. There is mentioned the gloating of enemies, a near death experience, falling short of the Lord's standard and personal repentance. All of this caused David to cry out, "Hear O Lord, and be merciful to me; O Lord, be my help." The psalm concludes with the note of gratitude, "You turned my wailing into dancing; you removed my sackcloth and clothed me with joy, that my heart may sing to you and not be silent. O Lord my God, I will give you thanks for ever."

The exciting part about the marriage dance is the way it survives age, illness, disability and separation. Because the dance steps are part of everyday living and the music plays in the heart, a married couple continue to dance to a rhythm and music unseen and unheard by others. The physical embrace may not be as strong, but the bonds which bind their hearts in love's embrace no earthly force can sever.

Reflect: How strongly, how clearly are we hearing Love's symphony in our relationship at this moment? Do I feel like dancing, or am I being a wall flower?

Prayer: The World wants me to listen to its cacophony and do my own steps, dear Lord. I long to hear the symphony of the Heavens and with my dancing partner embrace in Love's unending marriage dance.

Day 14
Kisses Sweeter than Wine

Reading: Song of Songs 7:1-13

Marriage can be likened to wine. There are high quality brands and cheap imitations. Both marriage and wine were meant for the benefit of men and women, yet too often bring ruin on careless, undisciplined participants. "God makes...wine that gladdens the heart of man, oil to make his face shine, and bread that sustains his heart" (Ps. 104:14, 15). In Ecclesiastes 9:7, 9 the writer links marriage and wine together: "Go, eat your food with gladness, and drink your wine with a joyful heart, for it is now that God favours what you do...Enjoy life with your wife, whom you love, all the days of this meaningless life that God has given you under the sun..." Most other passages mentioning wine do so with negative emphasis on its addictive powers.

A casual glance at marital statistics soon reveals a similar proportion. Too few couples discover and maintain the ongoing delights of marriage. As with wine, marriage should take on a deeper quality with age. For this to happen the whole process should start right from the beginning of the process. This requires the correct application of ingredients, preservatives and oversight to achieve the desired end. However, the most important ingredient in wine is the grape quality. So too, the greatest asset in marriage is the quality of the individual man and woman.

Both the wine and a marriage require the attention of an expert to bring out the best in both realms. Within marriage this belongs to the One who designed this relationship. God's desire is for couples to know the addiction of marital love in ever increasing delight. This comes about when a husband and wife, together and individually, allow the Lord to add those moral, spiritual additives and preservatives into their lives and relationship. It also requires personal initiatives to help keep the sparkle and the fizz from evaporating.

The book that expresses this so well is The Song of Songs. This love poem is included in Scripture as God's special ingredient and incentive for married couples to enrich their togetherness. Within its pages there are some interesting wine metaphors to gladden the hearts of lovers. It will keep you coming back for more and there isn't any hangover or regrets from indulging in it. Following are two passages to reflect upon. (read the whole book and find others.) One is from the woman's perspective, the other from the man's.

The wife's longing: "Let him kiss me with the kisses of his mouth– for your love is more delightful than wine. Pleasing is the fragrance of your perfumes; your name is like ointment poured forth" (Song of Songs 1:2, 3).

There are many wines with distinctive flavours. The kisses of a husband should also express the different distillation of a passionate heart.

The husband's desire:

> How delightful is your love, my sister, my bride! How much more pleasing is your love than wine, and the fragrance of your perfume than any spice! Your lips drop sweetness as the honeycomb, my bride; milk and honey are under your tongue. The fragrance of your garments is like that of Lebanon. You are a garden locked up, my sister, my bride; you are a spring enclosed, a sealed fountain. (Song of Songs 4:10-12)

It doesn't require much imagination to grasp how intoxicated this man was with his bride. That which would protect him from the grip of the grape would ever be to sip the wine from his wife's lips and to taste her sweetness. She was so nice to come home to!

The knowledge of this is beautifully expressed near the end of the poem when she appreciates the effect she has on her man and his commitment to her. In chapter 8:10b is a precious gem all married couples should unearth in their relationship: "Thus I have become in his eyes like one bringing contentment."

Reflect: How addicted am I to my spouse? How do I express my intoxication for him/her?

Prayer: Lord God, Creator and preserver of marriage, thank you for your love poem endorsing your approval on romantic love within marriage. May I give attention to how my lips express my heart when they meet the one you have given me to love, honour and cherish. Amen.

Day 15
A Sporting Affair

Reading: Song of Songs 2:1-17

The Bible is a passionate book dealing with real life people in real life situations and relationships. When you read some accounts it is evident rather bland words are used for certain sexual details. This is called 'euphemism' and means using a mild or indirect expression instead of a hard or unpleasant term.

"Abimelech king of the Philistines looked down from a window and saw Isaac caressing his wife Rebekah" (Genesis 26:8). In the KJV the word for caressing is 'sporting'. To fully understand the intensity of this caressing you need to see the association of the Hebrew word in Exodus 32:6: "The people rose up early and sacrificed burnt offerings and presented fellowship offerings (to an idol). Afterwards they sat down to eat and drink and got up to indulge in revelry (sport, play)."

The Lord God breathed into Adam passionate life. In the Garden of Eden such passion was controlled by righteousness and a Godly atmosphere. This all changed when Adam made the wrong move which resulted in an act of treason called Sin. Now passion became the driving force of the unrighteous soul. The apostle John sums it up in 1John 2:16: "Everything in the world – the cravings of sinful man, the lust of his eyes and boasting of what he has and does – comes not from the Father but from the world." This evil gang of three promotes its wares with great skill and sophistication to entice people into its slavery. What they don't make known is the fact such a life style ends in moral, spiritual and marital death.

Jesus faced this gang of three in the wilderness where He was tempted by the Devil. When you read Matthew 4 it is clear what the god of this world offered Jesus were these three soulish cravings of fallen human nature. Jesus even in His weakened state from forty days of fasting fended off this temptation. The way He did it is recorded in the words, "Away from me Satan! For it is written: 'Worship the Lord your God, and serve him only'." Coupled with that Jesus also said, "Man does not live by bread alone, but on every word that comes from the mouth of God." Here Jesus reveals how a man or woman can break the hypnotic spell of lust, craving and boasting, how to break free from the playground of death.

The result? A man is delivered from the snares of death: (Proverbs 14:27). Being set free from such snares a married couple can make their marriage a wonderful sporting affair played without regret and where both win.

A father recorded some advice he gave to his son. The young man was apparently preparing to be married. What is said is good, healthy encouragement for the prospective groom to delight in his wife. It is well worth reading in Proverbs 5:7-23. Two verses in particular are incentives to engage in a 'sporting' encounter: "May your fountain be blessed, and may you rejoice in the wife of your youth. A loving doe, a graceful deer – may her breasts satisfy you always, and may you ever be captivated by her love" (Proverbs 5:18-19).

One of the marvellous features about being sporty in marriage is the fact of age being no barrier. Have a peep into Abraham's biography. Sure, the athleticism of youth gives way to the more leisurely pursuits but the rules of engagement remain the same. The world weary writer of Ecclesiastes penned, "Enjoy life with your wife, whom you love…" (Ecclesiastes 9:9). Enjoyment, with your spouse, covers a whole range of activities in which pleasure is given and received! The only limitation is the imagination, or maybe the bank balance. The latter shouldn't be allowed to rob a husband and wife of enjoying each other. One Christmas a young, struggling family were unable to afford any worthwhile presents. What they did was cut out presents they would like to have given, sealed them in a card with a love letter. There was the promise that in better days the presents would be honoured. Christmas was a lovely time, thanks to the imagination.

Christmas was a time of love, thanks to each enjoying the other as God intended.

Reflect: Have I a game plan for expressing my enjoyment in my partner in our marriage? How would I describe it to him/her?

Prayer: May my love for my wife (husband) express the warmth of affection and the strength of commitment. I pray our love will always be within the umbrella of your grace and continue to be a joyous discovery of each other. Amen.

Day 16
The Husband's Role Model

Reading: Ephesians 5:22-33

Role models are meant to inspire. When we were young we had our sporting or adventure hero who motivated us to similar feats. As we matured and fell in love, where would we look for inspiration and motivation to be the best possible husband or wife? Unfortunately, there are too few heroes from our childhood with such credentials.

To be a good husband doesn't come naturally. The various factors associated with this role are rarely considered before the wedding service. Even if they were reviewed to any depth, the magic spell of being married would make it appear too easy. Then, after the honeymoon, reality knocks loud and clear.

Once again our Almighty Lord and Saviour did not leave you to lurch around in a frantic search for being a godly husband. The directives in the chosen reading are based upon His treatment of the Church.

The first feature to notice from the reading about Christ's example for husbands is about headship. This nearly always causes hassles to a husband and wife and for entirely different reasons. Headship isn't domination. It doesn't imply inferiority. It reflects responsibility under God. In the passage Jesus continues to make the Church beautiful. Herein abides the power of love. A husband's treatment of his wife over the years is to make her more beautiful. The wonder of such a love is the radiance of the relationship expressed in voice, eyes and nearness.

In Ephesians 5:28-29 the husband is to feed and care for his bride as though she was his own body. The illustration is highlighting the role Christ does for the Church. Therefore, the husband must seek to be the same for his wife. What are ways in which a man can fulfil this Christ-like calling in the intense environment of married life?

In God's estimation a husband is responsible for the atmosphere within the home. He can delegate but not abdicate. Leadership in the home is a prerequisite for leadership within a local congregation: "He must manage his own family well and see that his children obey him with proper respect" (1Timothy 3:4). The idea behind the word manage signifies the husband standing before the family, being up-front, implementing the decisions reached and accepting the repercussions. He shields the wife and any children. He also shares the blessings.

Joshua was a great leader and soldier. There is little mention about his wife and family. Where they are mentioned throws into stark contrast his priorities and those of many a man today Being a respected and successful leader, as he retired from national life, Joshua issued a challenge: "If serving the Lord seems undesirable to you, then choose for yourselves this day whom you will serve…But as for me and my household, we will serve the Lord" (Joshua 24:15).

The mouth is an instrument of exalting a wife, or crushing her. As a husband in his duty of care, what he says and how he says it is of utmost importance. The general admonition of Ephesians 4:29 is of particular relevance between a husband and wife: "Do not let any unwholesome talk come out of your mouth, but only what is helpful for building others up according to their needs, that it may benefit those who listen."

There are many other ways to consider the nourishing care of a husband for his wife. The incentive isn't only the Lord's example. It is also motivated by seeing the results in the wife. There is a radiance, a devotion, a passion and a delight evident in her attitude towards her husband. This is a beauty years can never erase.

In Proverbs 20:28 a statement concerning a king and the security of his throne is made: "Love and faithfulness keep a king safe; through love his throne is made secure." From the Biblical understanding a king was supposed to be guided by the Law of the Lord for the welfare of his subjects. If king was replaced with 'husband' the application of that verse to his marital standing and home environment would be realised.

Reflect: Is my leadership nourishing or stifling my wife's spiritual, emotional and creative roles?

Prayer: Lord, I open my heart to you. Fill it please with the food and vitamins needed to share with my wife. I stretch out my hands, asking you to bless them for I want my hands to care for and bless the lady you have given me as my wife. Thank you for her. Amen.

Day 17
Role Model for Wife

Reading: Ephesians 3:1-12

Women of renown, such as Ruth, Esther, Sarah and Mary could be on a short list as role models for women. Each warrants attention. However, the one chosen in the New Testament to inspire wives is the Church. The Ephesians letter portrays the highest and greatest romantic relationship as being between Christ and the Church. It is easy to focus upon Jesus because of His life story. The Church is more intangible, more mystical, even more difficult to describe. She is highlighted by Paul as the one best suited to unveil the role of a wife to her husband.

"His (God's) intent was that now, through the Church, the manifold wisdom of God should be made known to the rulers and authorities in the heavenly realms, according to his eternal purpose which he accomplished in Christ Jesus our Lord" (Ephesians 3:10, 11). A Christian wife in her relationship to her husband reveals God's wisdom. This happens as she seeks to know the Heavenly Father's purposes and obeys.

In a society of arranged marriages it must have been difficult for a man and woman to adjust to each other. The inevitable clash of personalities and upbringing would produce misunderstandings and resentments. The wisdom of God through the woman is bound up in the words "wives submit to your husbands as to the Lord." This much maligned aspect of the relationship actually is God's way of protecting and empowering the woman. The older, godly women are encouraged to assist the younger ones to love their husbands, exercise self-control (possibly with the tongue) and be pure. They are to manage their homes and express kindness. All is within the shadow of placing themselves under the gracious authority of their husband. The motivating factor is to prevent anyone from maligning the word of God. (Titus 2:4-5)

Within the passage devoted to marriage and singleness in perilous times, the Apostle Paul makes some astute observations. He says, "A married woman is concerned about the affairs of this world – how she can please her husband" (1Corinthians 7:34b). Her respect and blossoming love for her husband seeks to equip him as best she can to handle the pressures placed upon him outside the home. In a sexually promiscuous society what is written in 1 Corinthians 7:2-5 is sound advice: "Do not deprive each other except by mutual consent and for a time, so that you can devote yourselves to prayer: Then come together again so that Satan will not tempt you because of your lack of self-control" (verse 5).

In Ephesians 1:19-22 is a wonderful prayer for opening our understanding about the power and grace of God in Christ Jesus. It says that the exalting of Christ far above all authority, powers and dominions was for the Church to do. It is as if the Lord Jesus, after purchasing His bride through His poured out life, wanted her to be included in the enjoyment and promotion of His victory. The Church does this by honouring Her Lord through faithfulness and grace. Apply this into a husband and wife setting. The discipline of submission will be overshadowed by the sharing in the glory. The Church through her character and calling brings glory to her Lord and Saviour and thereby to the Heavenly Father (Ephesians 3:20-21). So too the wife in a similar manner honours the Almighty God as she honours her husband and shares in his joy and success.

To suggest this calling of the Church and by example the wife is easy misses the truth. It takes all the resources of God the Holy Spirit to enable a wife to place herself under the headship of her husband. He should exercise this responsibility with wisdom and consideration of his wife. The consequences for her, the husband and any children given will be more than worth the effort. When Jesus said He would build His church (Matthew 16:18) He implied giving His attention and time to it. Applying this principle to the husband will see him do likewise to his wife.

Using the Church as the role model for a woman in marriage lifts this relationship into the realm of the eternal, the beautiful and the unique.

Reflect: As a wife how do I understand "submission?" Do I honour my husband for whom he is as well as his God given role?

Prayer: I have to confess, Lord, there are times I cannot agree with my husband. Please help us to discuss these differences of opinion in a calm and productive way. Help us to submit to each other as your Word urges us to do. For those times we continue to disagree, I know it is my role to honour and obey him as the man you have given me for my husband. My independent nature makes this hard but I want to obey your Word. Please deepen our love for each other. Help us to honour You always in our marriage. Amen.

Day 18
The House Jesus Abides In

Reading: Hebrews 3:1-6

There's a beautiful picture of the artist Holman Hunt's impression of Jesus standing outside a closed door. He is knocking, seeking admission to the house with no external doorknob or key slot. It is bolted within. This work of art is taken from Revelation 3:20: "Here I am! I stand at the door and knock. If anyone hears my voice and opens the door I will come in and eat with him, and he with me."

There are a number of applications to this verse and all are important. In the context of a married couple's relationship and home building there is also an important principle. Jesus is no 'gate-crasher' nor will He huff and puff to blow the door down. He knocks. He calls out your name. He waits, but not indefinitely.

Within the Gospels we read of Jesus being invited into a number of homes. As you consider them it becomes apparent people can treat Jesus in their homes in various ways. Luke 7 records Him being in a prominent person's home but He was neglected by not receiving the common courtesies of the Day Jesus never made a fuss about it; instead, as the proper moment came around He used it to reveal the heart of the host. So different is the occasion in John 12 where the Lord is the guest of honour in the house of Lazarus, Mary and Martha. In verse 3 it says, "Then Mary took about a pint of pure nard, an expensive perfume; she poured it on Jesus' feet and wiped his feet with her hair. And the house was filled with the fragrance of the perfume." Devotion and gratitude for her Lord and friend motivated Mary to honour Him.

Jesus is treated the same way today in the spiritual dimension of a faith relationship. Within the home Jesus is either taken for granted and neglected, or honoured as Lord and friend. The spiritual and ethical atmosphere of the house will reflect whether His company is felt as a privilege, an imposition, or simply ignored.

The writer of Hebrews expresses the fact that when a person accepts Jesus Christ as Saviour and Lord he or she is indwelt by His presence. We are His dwelling place. In the experience of a married couple the Lord is in their midst. Together in the unity of love they form the household faith. This does not mean they are free from the trials and tribulations of life. Jesus makes this very clear in the parable of the two houses in Matthew 7:24-27. Two builders constructed similar houses but on two entirely different foundations. The same testing situations struck both houses. The one built on the sand collapsed under pressure. The one built on the rock was secure. "Therefore, everyone who hears these words of mine and puts them into practice is like the wise man who built his house on the rock" (verse 24). Do we believe it? Are we putting it into practice? The apostle Paul assures us also in 1 Corinthians 10:13, "God is faithful; he will not let you be tempted beyond what you can bear. But when you are tempted, he will also provide a way out so that you can stand up under it."

Establishing a house and home requires commitment and concentration. "By wisdom a house is built, and through understanding it is established; through knowledge its rooms are filled with rare and beautiful treasures" (Proverbs 24:3, 4). The treasures inferred are not trinkets, ornaments, or dazzling objects; rather they are things of unfading beauty and worth. Such things are love, integrity, faithfulness, respect, truth, joy and laughter, holiness and health. Proverbs 15:6 reminds us that "the house of the righteous contains great treasure" regardless of whether the couple live in a tent, shack or mansion.

Obed-Edom and his family were entrusted by King David with minding the Ark of the Covenant which he placed in their house. The ark was the expression of the presence of God and for three months it resided with Obed-Edom's family. A lovely comment is made in 2 Samuel 6:11: "…and the Lord blessed him and his entire household." Here is a principle to cling to. We do not have the Ark of the Covenant but we do have the guarantee of the Lord's presence in our household. How we treat His unseen presence will determine whether or not we, and our household, enjoy the blessing.

Reflect: How comfortable do I imagine Jesus is in my house? How natural am I in the knowledge of His presence in my life? How does my household view our invisible guest from watching my attitudes and actions?

Prayer: I remember the day you came into my life, Lord Jesus, and I have rejoiced in your faithfulness and companionship. May I express my gratitude to you in a manner reflecting the heart of Mary and her anointing of your feet. Cause my house to be permeated by the fragrance of your presence and a testimony to your grace. Amen.

Day 19
Love's Real Perfume (1)

Reading: Galatians 5:22-6:9

Perfumes capture the senses. "Perfume and incense bring joy to the heart" (Proverbs 27:9). It is a fragrant lasso thrown to hold and entice the one loved and desired. Such fragrances are used by those with the highest or the lowest of motives. The problem with such enticing aromas is their temporary nature. Before long, especially in the heat of the day, their aroma fades and the natural odours of the body seep through.

Within marriage the atmosphere created and enhanced in the words: "perfumed with myrrh and incense made from the spices of the merchant" (Song of Songs 3:6) is enthralling. However, if the soul nature of the husband and wife are out of harmony no amount of extraneous camouflage will suffice. The real fragrance of love comes from within. It has spiritual components wonderfully mixed and endlessly available for the needs of the one loved.

In the Galatians passage the source and components of Love's perfume is revealed. It is called "The Fruit of The Spirit." As you briefly consider the various aspects of it, keep this in mind: what is offered is for the benefit of the other. Just as a fruit tree produces fruit for the satisfaction of others, so too the "Fruit of The Spirit" within and from our lives is for others. This is the Holy Spirit's intention for His fruitfulness in the husband and the wife for their mutual satisfaction and marital health.

Joy is the first mentioned ingredient for Love's perfume. So closely allied in Greek to Grace it would appear you cannot have one without the other. Joy survives in the harshest of circumstances due to the grace of God. In Habakkuk 3:18, after describing rural catastrophes, he writes, "Yet I will rejoice in the Lord, I will be joyful in God my Saviour." Within marriage there will be various boulders crashing down upon a couple's love. It is the Lord's joy feeding on His promises which soften or deflect any falling boulders.

Peace is the next added spice. This doesn't mean the absence of strife from outside the walls. The term implies inner unity, concord. Because you are in unity with each other and with God, peace's spice combines with joy to bless your other half. "The mind controlled by the Spirit is life and peace" (Romans 8:6). Peace is a God given spice, which is added to an individual's heart open to God's Word. When the wife is being unsettled by events inside or outside the household how reassuring it is for her to breathe in the calmness of her husband's inner confidence.

Patience combines with the first two for a much needed and practical ingredient to the fragrance. In the KJV the word longsuffering is used. It's living in the era of the instant fix or the demand for the immediate that tends to make us impatient with everything and everyone. How sad this short fused approach to life is seen in the unwillingness to carry the load or enduring the other person's pain. God weaves into Love's real perfume this aromatic herb with the power to offer support, strength and grace within the tiring circumstances being experienced. This isn't an easy herb to blend with the other two. Skill with determination must be exercised. Writing from prison to the Church at Ephesus Paul said, "I urge you to live a life worthy of the calling you have received. Be completely humble and gentle; be patient, bearing with one another in love" (Ephesians 4:1-2).

Kindness must be added to patience lest a sense of bitterness and fatalism sneaks in and makes the perfume of Love stink. How can you be kind when your surroundings are intent upon hardening you or corrupting your relationship? This is only possible when you understand how Christ Jesus considered you. The World will harden you. Christ will keep you tender and safeguard your integrity. Remember Titus 3:4: "When the kindness and love of God our Saviour appeared, he saved us, not because of righteous things we had done, but because of his mercy." Within Love's eternal perfume kindness is a most favoured and value added ingredient.

Tomorrow the remaining additives will be considered. When all are combined there is such a strong touch of Heaven about the fragrance of love.

Reflect: Out of the four components considered of which do I need the Lord to increase the supply? How will He do it?

Prayer: Lord, I'm a little short on some of the spices mentioned and I come to you to be re-supplied. Having no funds to purchase them I would place them on my Saviour's account and in gratitude use them as He directs. Amen.

Day 20
Love's Real Perfume (2)

Reading: 2 Corinthians 2:12-3:6

Expensive fragrances in Roman days were often stored in clay vessels. Over time the vessels would become permeated by the perfume stored. Even when the vessel was broken the aroma contained would be spread abroad. In the reading it is evident Paul compared the vessels with the Believer's total being. The Corinthians became aware of this when they read, "We have this treasure in jars of clay to show that this all-surpassing power is from God and not from us" (2 Corinthians 4:7).

The Holy Spirit makes the perfume of Heaven for the life of a believer and pours it into the heart through the channel of faith. In the previous devotion four spices were considered as comprising part of the perfume's mixture. The next one considered is the spice of *goodness*. Scripture informs that only God is good and from that we all fall short. The goodness within the fragrance points to an individual's desire to be moral, righteous, true and generous. In Matthew 20:1-15 is the parable of workers in the vineyard. At the end of the day the owner gave the same reward to those who had laboured a much shorter time than others. Confronting the criticisms the master said, "Are you envious because I am generous?" (verse 15). In the Greek the word 'generous' is good. By our Lord's generosity goodness is defined. What a stimulating ingredient this spice adds to Love's perfume.

Faithfulness is added to the mix making the perfume strong to the senses of the lover. When a person exudes trustworthiness to another it literally makes love feel secure. Within marriage this spice is the one which binds all the others together. The aroma put forth repels the seductive, blunts the offensive and strengthens the will-power. The truth of Proverbs 25:13 is amply borne out between a man and wife: "Like the coolness of snow at harvest time is a trustworthy messenger to those who send him; he refreshes the spirit of his masters."

"By the meekness and *gentleness* of Christ I appeal to you..." (2 Corinthians 10:1) wrote Paul. The word gentleness in Galatians 5:23 is describing Christ's character as being meek. Far from being a weakness this additive to Love's perfume enhances its whole composition. Meekness provides the soft answer to injurious words yet is able to stand up and defend against the unjust and the untrue. The husband is more likely to need a strong dose of this spice within his spiritual fragrance to combat the world's stress upon the macho man. His wife draws closer to him through this strong, vibrant, yet soft scent of true manliness more than any show of brute power. A self description by Jesus is one all Christians should desire, none more so than married couples. Only the indwelling presence of the Lord Jesus can make it possible. How wonderful would Love's perfume flavour the words of a spouse to the wearied partner, "Come to me…you who are weary and burdened, and I will give you rest…learn from me, for I am gentle (meek KJV) and humble in heart" (Matthew 11:28,29).

Self-control is the final ingredient. When blended the combination is the most alluring, fascinating and spellbinding perfume to flow from the inner being of a man or woman. In a society promoting no restraint, especially in the moral realm, this spice is one often frowned upon. The outworking of this final additive has the effect of the husband putting the needs of his wife before his own. It controls the wife's sense of her rights in favour of pleasing her husband. The word is linked with righteousness and knowledge. Righteousness comes from God therefore self-control is the person's acceptance and application of God's righteousness within his/her life. However, personal discipline requires knowledge lest it decays into negative and narrow attitudes to life, family and godliness. Rightly applying God's word and righteousness to personal situations will protect self-control becoming rigor mortis in the soul.

Love's real perfume isn't cheap. It is actually priceless. The wonder of the Triune God's mercy is He bestows it freely to faithful, obedient, hungry-hearted believers. No married couple should live without it.

Reflect: Who paid the cost of Heaven's perfume? Of course it is Christ! How am I unleashing His fragrance each day? Do I need replenishing?

Prayer: Am I a strong fragrance of your Grace beloved Lord? May I be a vessel through which your perfume flows to others, but most especially to my wife/husband so that she/he may be saturated by Heaven's aroma. Amen.

Day 21
Recovering Love

Reading: Revelation 2:1-5

The Church is pictured as being the Bride of Christ (Ephesians 5:22-33). This has been considered in a previous devotional. In reading the passage in Revelation it becomes evident there is something missing between Christ and the Church. Outwardly things appear very attractive but the Lord knows the heart.

Husbands and wives do not have the capacity to see the unseen depths of each other's hearts and minds. However there is an awareness which creeps upon the relationship. Something is lacking despite material comfort, interesting adventures and pleasures. Love seems to have faded, been subverted or taken a holiday. Left in that condition it will suffer the same sadness as the 'candlestick' in the reading:

Where Does Love Go?

Where does love go
when it is tired,
weary from trying,
wasted from giving,
where does it go?
I need to follow it
beg it
to return.

What does love do
wherever it goes?
Can it be healed,
find wholeness?
Where does it go?
I need to know,
help it
recover.

How does love know
it needs to leave,
sick, near death,
nothing left to give?
Where does it go?
I need to cry
for its
renewal.

Can love live again,
rediscover its joy,
relight frozen embers?
Can love breathe life
where it has gone?
I need to know
O Lord,
let it live.

Will love ever return,
embrace again
the one who crushed it
by selfish neglect?
Where should I go
to learn of love,
know it,
display it?

Who can renew love,
rebuild its trust,
safeguard its purity?
Before Him I would bow!
Where can I go?
The place I'm told
for Love
is Jesus!

Reflect: God is love, the Bible declares. It also says love flows from Him. The best guarantee against losing the passion of first love is undeniably linked with how a person stands with God.

Prayer: May I be diligent in guarding my love for my partner from the subtle seductions which pander to my nature. Lord, by your love ever refresh my love, passion and pride in the one you have given me. Amen.

Day 22

Happy Ever After (1)

Reading: Matthew 5:1-12

'Happy ever after' is the climax of many a fairy story. The longing of the human heart is such that the desire for happiness comes out even in children's stories. For many the longing remains just that, a longing. The Bible offers, not merely a happy ending, it also shows the way to a happy journey together. Within many translations the word 'happy' is rarely, if ever used. Instead, the word 'blessed' is preferred. To modern ears it sounds either strange or reserved for beatified saints. However it simply means to be happy, very happy.

Within the 150 Psalms the various writers saturate their compositions with the word, blessed. In many ways it is an expression of their encounters with Yahweh they wish to share with others. Happiness, from a Biblical viewpoint, can never remain a captive to an individual's selfishness. It must be shared.

Scripture doesn't ignore or camouflage the tough realities of married life. What it does promise is God's faithfulness and His Word's empowerment. This is sorely needed in the rough, unpleasant and sometimes cruel facets of living in a corrupt world. From the Biblical perspective, God given happiness wrestles with such intruders to prevail over them rather than allowing them to dominate. Therefore, to enjoy God given happiness within marriage means finding out how and where it is given.

At first glance it seems strange that happiness and fear are hand in hand in God's plans for individuals, couples, families and communities. Stranger still, one without the other becomes a mirage or an oppressive force. There are at least ten words in the Hebrew translated as fear. The one associated with knowing God given happiness points to a holy awe of the Eternal God. Such reverence means a person is motivated to take His words seriously. To be serious with God doesn't always mean it is easy or pleasant to put His Word into practice. However, similar to taking medicine for sickness, it produces health, and prevents moral and spiritual infections. Within marriage a mutual holy awe of God creates an atmosphere of grace, mercy and forgiveness.

"The fear of the Lord leads to life. Then one rests content, untouched by trouble" (Proverbs 19:23). This isn't saying troubles don't come knocking, even bombarding, your heart and mind. It means they do not bruise you, crush you or haunt you. Compare Paul's contentment in Philippians 4:10-13.

Fear is one of many repeated words in Proverbs, a book of practical insights to life. To a man it says, "The fear of the Lord teaches a man wisdom, and humility comes before honour" (15:33). To a woman it says, "Charm is deceptive, and beauty is fleeting; but a woman who fears the Lord is to be praised" (30:31). To a couple with children, "He who fears the Lord has a secure fortress, and for his children it will be a refuge" (14:26).

"Blessed are all who fear the Lord, who walk in his ways...your wife will be a fruitful vine within your house" (Psalm 128:1-3). Of course the same applies if the wife reads it and applies it to her husband. Why is this? Because the smile of God is upon them and He can overrule in the lives of those who trust Him even in the unfairness of life.

In Numbers 6:24 is a beautiful blessing. Yahweh wanted this to be said over the nation of Israel as they journeyed to the Promised Land. God knew His people had some severe trials ahead and wanted them to know faith and obedience to Him would always guarantee His favour: "The Lord bless you and keep you; the Lord make his face shine upon you and be gracious to you; the Lord turn his face towards you and give you peace."

When a man and woman unite their lives under God, He takes delight in them. Some couples know this from their wedding day For other couples it is a joyous truth discovered further down the marital road when they invite the Lord Jesus into their relationship. Happy ever after ceases to be an unfulfilled longing as the couple fear God and keep His word. From then on they experience the wonder of His blessing individually and become a blessing to each other, and to all who live in their shadow.

Reflect: "The Lord delights in those who fear him, who put their hope in his unfailing love" (Psalm 147:11).

Prayer: May I be awe struck by who you are and by what you have done to express your holiness and grace to humanity. I want, need, your blessing so who I am and what I do may bless my other half. Amen.

Day 23

Happy Ever After (2)

Reading: Isaiah 26:1-9

Within secular love songs can be found the echo of a sacred longing. It's as though the promise of Eden still permeates the heart of men and women. Think of your favourite love songs. Examine their words. Can you read words impregnated with Eden's hope? One I especially like is 'Love changes everything.' Two things strike me about that song. One is that I could sing it to the Lord and mean it. The second one, the words express what the love of my wife has aroused in my life with and for her. There are many other love songs that arouse similar emotions within my heart. What are some songs capable of creating similar experiences in your heart?

Why is there this haunting refrain within love songs arousing the sense of, and longing for, Heaven's presence? Is it due to the Bible describing God as Love? Creating Adam and Eve in His image would have saturated their total personality with His love. Seduced from trusting God, Adam and Eve lost the immediate and intimate presence of God. Whilst this loss distorted so much of Adam and Eve's relationship, the taste of true love never completely evaporated. It permeates our hearts and minds still. Many of the love songs written, even by those who reject the Biblical account and revelation of God, reflect this longing. Eden's love lingers. A hunger remains.

The unfortunate fact of life for so many is stated by Elihu in the disturbing book of Job: "Men cry out under a load of oppression; they plead for relief from the arm of the powerful. But no one says, 'Where is God my Maker, who gives songs in the night'...?" (Job 35:9-10). Everyone knows the world needs love and imagine it can be unearthed from one's own inner being. Human love dries up and the song fades in despair. So different are the songs composed in the atmosphere of God's love. "I will sing of the Lord's great love forever; with my mouth I will make your faithfulness known through all generations. I will declare that your love stands firm forever, that you have established your faithfulness in heaven itself" (Psalm 89:1-2).

When men and women link their lives by Faith to God they rediscover the source of True Love. It comes to them through Jesus Christ and His passion at Calvary. Love is the inheritance of faith testified to by the empty tomb. Love is the gift of God shed abroad in the hearts of the faithful by the Holy Spirit. The long lost sounds of Eden are found again in Christ Jesus. Men and women not only sense the longing in the secular songs, they taste the song's fulfilment through God's saving grace.

How does this apply to a marriage?

God has recorded a couple of love songs within Scripture. Using the imagery of marriage, the Lord sings the song of a broken heart in Isaiah 5. He married the Nation of Israel and she became unfaithful. As her husband He had to take unwelcome discipline and it saddened Him. Does the Lord understand and sympathise with those who suffer separation? Yes! He has a song of tears to share with that couple. He also has a song of hope. "I am now going to allure her; I will lead her into the desert and speak tenderly to her…In that day, declares the Lord, you will call me 'my husband'…" Hosea 2:14-16. In Zephaniah is the account of a marital relationship restored as both parties rejoice in song, "Sing, O Daughter of Zion; shout aloud, O Israel! Be glad and rejoice with all your heart O Daughter of Jerusalem" (Zephaniah 3:14.). The prophet picks up the majestic voice of God as He delights in His people and rejoices over them with singing (3:17).

When this takes place the song of love, as given in Eden, will be sung again. The longing of the secular will be enveloped in the sacred as originally designed. Until then we can taste Eden's promise within marriage by personal faith. To do that each needs to sing Psalm 101:1-2: "I will sing of your love and justice; to you O Lord, I will sing praise. I will be careful to lead a blameless life – when will you come to me? I will walk in my house with blameless heart. I will set before my eyes no vile thing."

Reflect: Am I singing and making melody to the Lord? Is it a solo or duet?

Prayer: When people look at my marriage, Heavenly Father, I pray they will see a duet but hear a trio. Amen.

Day 24

There's an Art to Knowing

Reading: Genesis 4:1, 1 Corinthians 7:3-5

I wonder what song Adam would have sung to Eve as they began their unique and precious relationship. My choice would be 'Getting to know you, getting to know all about you.' One thing is sure he didn't have to worry about her previous history. However, what was it that created such stirrings in his being when he looked at her? In Genesis 4:1 in the King James Version the word 'knew' is used to express the wonder of the sexual relationship. To us it may sound quaint yet it is a very expressive and insightful word to use for such an intimate experience.

Today when a man and woman marry and 'know' each other they have been conditioned simply to apply it to the physical act of intercourse. To live in that understanding is to walk your relationship into a wilderness of disappointment and shallowness. Getting to know each other is a journey of trust, and a privilege of commitment. For we each come into a marital relationship with unique histories, personalities, expectations and dreams many of which wait unearthing as love deepens.

The Bible tells us that we are body, soul and spirit. Each facet of who we are is involved in and colours that relationship woven in the word 'to know'. The surface feature is simple to grasp. The body is tangible, attractive and responsive up to a point. However love requires more than the physical. Loving embraces the person who expresses himself or herself through the flesh. Therefore as a husband understands, appreciates, admires and discovers more and more of his wife so his joy increases and his amazement abounds. The same of course applies to the wife's experience.

In Hosea 4:6 is a sad note in a sad love story portraying God's love for Israel in the life of Hosea and Gomer: "My people are destroyed from lack of knowledge." This is a summary of the breakdown in relationships. To adequately 'know' each other in its intense and wide meaning requires both to continue to explore the hidden realms of each other's heart and mind, history and hopes. The marital wilderness is littered with the 'skeletons' of ignorant couples whose sole concept of marriage was to take and enjoy the surface, the superficial, and ignore the spiritual and sublime.

The Apostle Peter in an important passage on marriage speaks to both wife and husband in 1 Peter 3:1-7. I think he must have lived this out in his own marriage, possibly in a more meaningful way after the resurrection of Jesus Christ and its personal effect on his relationship. The word to the husband in verse 7 – again from the KJV – says, "husbands dwell with them (wives) according to knowledge." Peter doesn't go into detail, which in a way is disappointing but at the same time stimulating to the reader's mind. How can I live under the same roof in a meaningful, Christ honouring way with the woman who shares my body, soul and spirit? Especially if it is further complicated with children, health issues and demands made by work?

Does this place both the man and the woman under an obligation not to take the other for granted, not to cease walking together in new discoveries, but to improve one's skills in understanding and sharing? Surely it does! Knowledge evaporates myth. Truth increases the mystery of the majestic.

Proverbs is a wonderful collection of insights gained from life and is as relevant for today as when penned. In the New International Version the wise man is called prudent. He is the opposite of the foolish and ignorant man. In 13:16 we are told that "every prudent man acts out of knowledge" and 24:3-5 says, "By wisdom a house is built, and through understanding it is established; through knowledge its rooms are filled with rare and beautiful treasures. A wise man has great power, and a man of knowledge increases strength." I like the implications of 'rooms are filled with rare and beautiful treasures' especially when applied to the room where a husband and wife 'know' each other.

Reflect: "The fear of the Lord is the beginning of knowledge, but fools despise wisdom and discipline" (Proverbs 1:7). In my present situation how would I rate in this simple gauge of my knowledge of my spouse?

Prayer: I would like the rooms of my heart as well as my home to be filled with rare and beautiful treasures for my lover, friend and partner. I long to be wise in understanding my spouse so as to love her with all my heart, mind, body and soul! Grant me an insatiable longing for knowledge that flows out of my reverence and commitment to you. I know then that my relationship with her will never be a skeleton in a marital waste land. Amen.

Day 25

God's Centre for Marriage Renewal

Reading: Psalm 100

Worship is always a personal experience even in the midst of a congregation. However, whether alone or in company, a person's bearing before the Lord is affected by his relationship to others. In the Sermon on the Mount Jesus said, "If you are offering your gift at the altar and there remember that your brother has something against you, leave your gift there in the front of the altar. First go and be reconciled to your brother; then come and offer your gift" (Matt. 5:23, 24).

Within the Christian Faith a similar condition applies. Holy Communion, the Lord's Supper or the Eucharist as it may be called presents the same demand. Every relationship comes under scrutiny by the Holy Spirit in this time of remembrance and celebration. The significance for a husband and wife relationship is obvious. As they share in Communion they do so as a unit not as individuals. Sitting there together before the light of God's Grace He searches their hearts to reveal any dark areas needing attention. Such dark spots may have appeared through neglect, abuse, or un-forgiveness. Should any of these attitudes be present then worship is seriously affected and the joy of the Lord to them is limited. In 1 Corinthians 11:17-34 failure to worship properly was given by the apostle Paul as the reason why many Corinthian believers were weak, sick or had died. The Church was challenged to take stock of themselves, their attitudes, as well as their treatment of each other. From the same foundation, a husband and wife need to constantly assess their relationship before the Lord. Failure to do this often explains why Christian marriages become sick, struggle or worse still, shatter.

The term Eucharist means 'Thanksgiving'. To participate in this act of taking the emblems of the body and blood of Jesus Christ is a wonderful way to express gratitude to God. It is also an opportunity for a husband to say thanks for his wife, and for her to do the same concerning her husband. Together they bow before their Redeemer and Lord, confessing His goodness and mercy. Here each is challenged by the testimony of the cross to offer a similar mercy and forgiveness to the other. Worship, especially in Communion, becomes an ongoing healing process and 'quality assurance' checklist for each couple. As James puts it, and here it is applied to marriage and worship, "With our tongue we praise our Lord and Father, and with it we curse men, who have been made in God's likeness. Out of the same mouth come praise and cursing. My brothers, this should not be" (James 3:9, 10). Our Lord sees the heart before He hears the words. Therefore it's vitally important for both hearts to be beating as one, free from animosity and unresolved hurts.

Communion provides for a couple ongoing avenues for romance. Being reminded of the Love of the Lord, expressed at Calvary, stirs up love for Him. As they respond to the One the Scriptures call Love, their own love is deepened, refreshed and motivated. It's impossible to spend time in the Lord's company with a genuine love for Him and not want to honour your spouse. Each couple should leave the worship service more in love than when they entered the place. How? As a result of not only meeting with the Lord but also dealing with issues He aroused in the mind. How gracious is our Lord and Saviour in providing such marital renewal opportunities within the context of remembering His death, burial and resurrection. No marriage need remain entombed in past failures or tears. The Lord's resurrection offers salvation, mercy and newness from personal sin and enslavement. He has resurrection power to apply to any marriage so it can live again. All He needs is permission to release it within the relationship.

"Let us consider how we may spur one another on towards love and good deeds. Let us not give up meeting together, as some are in the habit of doing, but let us encourage one another–and all the more as you see the Day approaching" (Hebrews 10:24-25). This is fantastic advice to married couples. The word 'spur' means to stimulate, motivate, to get the other on the move. The question arises, "How?" By applying the mind to understand the spouse's interests, needs and dreams! Then you must put some effort or guile in making it a reality. Too often married couples let the 'spurs' in the relationship fall off. When that happens, 'burrs' blow in.

The writer of Hebrews warns against absenteeism from worship. Why? Because the results are always negative for faith, testimony, stewardship and knowing the joy of the Lord! Within the realm of marriage, being absent without reason from worship is a form of self robbery! Absent Without Reason denies oneself of the Lord's renewing, healing and transforming grace. It also lessens the interest in wearing 'spurs'. Husbands and wives must be wary of limiting the possibilities for their marital health, adventure and romance.

Reflect: I'm not very creative or imaginative but I can learn. There are numerous resources available so I'll go check them out and see what spurs I can find.

Prayer: Eternal God you have given us an awesome privilege in worship, especially as a married couple. I want to thank you for Communion. You have, through this time, blessed my spouse and me over the years. It's been a constant source of renewal and encouragement. Thanks again. Amen.

Day 26

The Highest Quality of Love

Reading: 1 Corinthians 13:1-13

Is it written simply to taunt? Is it there to make us fear our inadequacy? It is, however, undoubtedly beautiful. Undeniably lovely in its intentions, it's nonetheless daunting to practise.

When a bride and groom have this passage spoken at their wedding they really desire for it to be realised. Married life quickly reveals the sad truth. The words of 1Corinthians 13 may be desirable but it's beyond the ability of either partner to maintain. Before long the ecstasy of the wedding vows gives way to the agony of weekday woes. Why do couples choose this majestic passage of Scripture about Love and imagine it's going to happen as if by magic?

The love that is stressed in this reading is actually best understood as Divine Love. That is, whilst humanly desired its actual source is outside the strength and stamina of the human heart. The Greek language at the time of the New Testament writings had four words for love. There was friendship love, family love, erotic love and this Agape or the Highest Love. It was so rare a quality in the experiences of men and women that the Church seized on it to define the Love of God. Therefore when the apostle used Agape in his letter to the Corinthian church he was using this word to explain the eternal and unconditional love of God.

"This is love (Agape); not that we loved God, but that he loved us and sent his Son as an atoning sacrifice for our sins" (1 John 4:10). It becomes evident such love initiates action for the welfare of the one loved and is willing to pay the price. This love, wrapped in sacrifice, is portrayed in the human arena by "Greater love has no one than this, that he lay down his life for his friends" (John 15:13). What Jesus spoke about was the pinnacle of human love. He went further. He gave His life even for His enemies (see Romans 5: 6-11).

What are the implications for a married couple long after the wedding service? Each has made a vow to offer such love to the other. Each was required to let it flow to the other, whether he or she deserves it or not. A soldier might give his life to save his friend in the heat of battle. Such action deserves recognition and reward. There is a sense, however, in which a husband or wife are expected to regularly 'give up' his or her life for the welfare of the other. It is a living sacrifice being offered. What can happen is best said by Jesus when He spoke to His disciples in the upper room on Passover night: "As I have loved you, so you must love one another. By this all men will know that you are my disciples, if you love one another" (John 13:34, 35). When lived out within marriage others become aware such sacrificial love is not considered drudgery but the greatest expression of being in love. That doesn't make it any the less demanding but love transforms it into a gift to the one loved.

How then can this highest love take root in a marriage? The best way to illustrate this comes from Psalm 1: (The term 'man' has been changed to couple for obvious reasons.) "Blessed is the couple... whose delight is in the law of the Lord, and on His law they meditate day and night. They are like a tree planted by streams of water, which yields its fruit in season and whose leaf does not wither. Whatever they do prospers...for the Lord watches over the way of the righteous couple." The word for streams means one which has been painstakingly dug so as to irrigate the planted tree.

Any form of the four loves requires an irrigation channel to be dug so the waters can flow. This is the individual's responsibility, not God's. Both need to dig and maintain the channel and delight themselves in the Lord. It can be done, by either the husband or wife, but requires greater effort and perseverance going solo. God is faithful. He will cause the waters of love to flow. This water will cause the 'marriage tree' to blossom and bear fruit even in the drought times of life. The Lord made a promise to Israel in Isaiah 58:11: "The Lord will guide you always; he will satisfy your needs in a sun-scorched land and will strengthen your frame. You will be like a well-watered garden, like a spring whose waters never fail." The principle of which can be applied to the spiritual life of all God's people.

Reflect: Have I been digging any irrigation channels lately for the waters of love to flow? How well maintained are the ones already dug?

Prayer: You, Lord, are the giver of the water of life. Let it flow within my marriage I pray. Deal with any blockage in my heart and help me to use love's spade to dig some new channels for Agape's refreshing waters to flow to my other half. Amen.

Day 27

Keeping Marriage Holy

Reading: 1Thessalonians 4:1-8

Seahorses are intriguing creatures. Breeding them commercially requires guarding against infection and feeding appropriate food. Being in large tubs there is a build up of body waste and uneaten food. If left unattended the accumulation of ammonia and bacteria would ultimately kill them. It is essential the dirt be removed from the tank and a constant circulating of water be maintained for their well being.

Within your personal life and marriage a similar principle applies. Each day, immoral dirt accumulates and combines with unwholesome attitudes and festering feelings. These threaten personal well-being and marital wholeness. There is a need for someone or something to siphon from the heart and mind the filth of the world and the perverse enjoyment of the sinful nature.

God in His mercy set out principles for the welfare of His people. In the Old Testament are laws and statutes, especially those concerned with a pilgrim people. In them you'll find some very basic safeguards for the prevention of plague and communal discomfort. Deuteronomy 23:12-14 is an example: "Designate a place outside the camp where you can go and relieve yourself. As a part of your equipment have something to dig with, and when you have relieved yourself, dig a hole and cover up your excrement. For the Lord your God moves about in your camp to protect you and deliver your enemies to you. Your camp must be holy, so that he will not see among you anything indecent and turn away from you."

This very practical requirement was based on the character of the Creator and Redeemer God. It also stresses the fact His presence is affected by the way His people deal with anything which pollutes. It doesn't take much effort to see how this applies to personal living and marital relationships.

When you surrendered your life to Jesus Christ as Lord and Saviour He cleansed you from all the pollution and corruption of Sin. "The blood of Christ, who through the eternal spirit offered himself unblemished to God, cleanse(d) our consciences from acts that lead to death, so that we may serve the living God" (Hebrews 9:14). He separated you from the past and linked you with Himself. When you were married, the Lord Jesus joined you both together 'in Him'. This marital relationship is separate and distinct from the world's understanding of wedlock. However the corruption within your realm of living plus a soul nature which leans heavily towards self indulgent and unholy behaviour means you need regular 'siphoning'. God has provided such a health saving instrument, namely, His Word. By prayer and His Word you can deal with the rubbish, which would otherwise stifle your spiritual and moral life.

In 1 Thessalonians 4:3-5 is an interesting section dealing with being sanctified. The word means being distinct from the World's morality. "It is God's will that you should be sanctified: that you should avoid sexual immorality, that each of you should learn to control his own body in a way that is holy and honourable, not in passionate lust like the heathen who do not know God." In the margin is the suggestion the term body could refer to wife. In the Greek it simply uses the word 'vessel' with the implication it refers to the wife. Of course from the woman's view the same applies for the man. It is a directive for each to treat the other in a holy and special manner and to allow nothing from past lifestyle or present community values to corrupt it.

Keeping the marriage bed pure (Hebrews 13:4) is the incentive for sanctification, the blessing of God, the testimony of grace to any children and the prevention of any ghosts of regret. When holiness in God's sight is a personal reality then unsullied passion is the gift a husband and wife offer each other.

God's will and Word are the foundation for a fulfilled and satisfying life. He has recorded for you the principles to deal with the dirt which lodges in the soul. "Since we have these promises, dear friends, let us purify ourselves from everything that contaminates body and spirit, perfecting holiness out of reverence for God" (2 Corinthians 7:1).

Reflect: How well do I know the promises of God to deal with the dirt of the past and that which flies around in the present?

Prayer: I want to make the prayer of David from Psalm 51 my own, beloved God. Have mercy on me, O God, according to your unfailing love; according to your great compassion blot out my transgressions. Wash away all my iniquity and cleanse me from my sin. Amen.

Day 28
Cultivating Marriage

Reading: Psalm 128

"Your wife will be like a fruitful vine within your house" (Ps.128:3) is a promise to those who fear the Lord and walk in His ways. The wife is being honoured by the image of a vine. If you live in a grape growing and wine making area you will readily gain the significance of the title. The wife is considered a valuable asset well worth guarding and nourishing. The responsibility of the husband is implied rather than stated. Would it be far from the mark to say, from the wife's perspective, the husband is also a fruitful vine? Accepting this, marriage can be visualized as a boutique vineyard producing the fruit of the vine, a symbol of love's intoxication.

A vineyard requires good management and care if it is to reach its full potential. Neglect of the vine is a tragedy plus a waste of the fruit. Consider Proverbs 24:30-32: "I went past the field of the sluggard, past the vineyard of the man who lacks judgment; thorns had come up everywhere, the ground was covered with weeds, and the stone wall was in ruins. I applied my heart to what I observed and learned a lesson from what I saw."

Happy marriages do not happen as if by magic. They are planned, managed and enjoyed. A wedding may have Heaven's blessing yet end up being cursed on earth due to indolence, indulgence and ignorance by one or both partners. Unless good intentions motivate to finding true wisdom, marriage, similar to a vineyard, will simply fall into disrepair. "It is not good to have zeal without knowledge, and nor to be hasty and miss the way" (Proverbs 19:2).

In Biblical times vineyards were guarded by hedges designed to protect them from foxes, jackals and thieves. If breached, the intruders must be dealt with. "Catch for us the foxes, the little foxes that ruin the vineyards, our vineyards that are in bloom" (Song of Songs 2:15). The trouble with little foxes is they grow. Eradicate them before they multiply and do extensive damage. How would you discern the threat of moral and spiritual foxes creeping towards your marital relationship? Sometimes they come disguised as good things yet their intent is to breach the walls.

What type of marital hedge would you construct to safeguard your marriage? The following four sides join together to surround your marriage and keep it safe!

Side one: Worship the Lord together. He is the best hedge repairer, constructor and maintainer. Worship keeps you focused on Him. It allows Him to speak to your heart about areas needing attention. "Come, let us bow down in worship, let us kneel before the Lord our Maker" (Psalm 95:6).

Side two: Prayer: Individually is a must, together is delightful but not always possible. This form of communication is coloured by personality and circumstances. "God has surely listened and heard my voice in prayer: Praise be to God, who has not rejected my prayer or withheld his love from me" (Psalm 66:19-20). There are also many good books available for you to buy, read and apply on this subject.

Side three: Time together. One of the hedge demolishing tricks of the world is to prevent husband and wife from spending regular time together. Lovers need to be alone. To be alone together requires strategies and determination. A cost may be involved; the rewards however exceed it over and over again.

Side four: Surprises. Never take the other for granted. Do things out of the ordinary. They need not be elaborate or costly. Keep it simple. Make it fun. The great thing about surprising your wife or husband is the way the pleasure is shared.

Reflect: Have I inspected the hedges around my vineyard lately? Is there any area being neglected?

Prayer: I come to you, Beloved Lord, to seek wisdom in understanding the needs of my vineyard. May I nourish, guard and care for my spouse so we together may enjoy the fruits of our marriage. Amen.

Day 29
The Bride

Reading: Isaiah 62:1-12

The giving of Eve to Adam in Genesis 2 was a shadow of a greater giving and receiving. As marriage was ordained by God the Father, Son and Holy Spirit, its meaning, majesty and mystique flow from His intentions. Sin's rebellion has sought to corrupt or cancel out the significance of Biblical commitment in marriage.

Israel was chosen by Yahweh to be His bride. Within this covenant relationship Israel was to honour Him and be the one through whom the Messiah would come. The thirty-nine books of the Old Testament reveal God's faithfulness and Israel's unfaithfulness. Read Ezekiel 16 for a graphic insight into this. In the book of Hosea is the story of a husband and wife who portray Israel's spiritual history. Gomer's unfaithfulness and Hosea's love which kept seeking after her became a portrayal of God's love for Israel, and also for us.

The reading in Isaiah penetrated the future to the time when God reclaims His unfaithful wife through redemption and mercy (compare Ezekiel 36-38). In Isaiah 53 is the price of reclaiming and purifying the unfaithful nation: "For the transgression of my people he was stricken" (verse 8b). Why did He bother? For at least two reasons! One relates to His faithfulness. When the Lord God entered into a Covenant with Israel it was forever. In our marriage ceremony the phrase "Until death do us part" was to mean just that within the marriage commitment. God cannot die. Therefore His promise is eternal. (Romans 11:29.) The Bride has wandered away but the Husband is pursuing her as highlighted in Hosea. We Gentiles once excluded from citizenship in Israel and the Covenants have been included in this redemptive plan. That's grace (see Ephesians 2).

Today the World looks with disdain on the unfaithful bride, Israel, and calls her the deserted one. Speaking through the prophet the voice of God is heard: "No longer will they call you Deserted, or name your land Desolate. But you will be called Hephzibah and your land Beulah" (Isaiah 62:4). Hephzibah means, 'my delight is in her.' Combining the name with the nation is a declaration concerning the one some consider less than Cinderella. In Yahweh's purposes she is destined to reign. How appropriate. She who had become lost, forlorn and abandoned is to experience the Lord of Glory coming to reclaim her for Himself. "Then you will know that I, the Lord, am your Saviour, your Redeemer, the Mighty One of Jacob" (Isaiah 60:16).

A second reason is found in Ezekiel 36:22: "This is what the Sovereign Lord says: It is not for your sake, O house of Israel, that I am going to do these things, but for the sake of my holy name." If God simply abandoned His covenant due to human and national weakness, why would He have entered into it in the first place? He knows the future and invested His Name in and over the nation He chose to call His Bride. The implications for us are also resting on His ability to fulfil His word. Is the Church any more pure, faithful and committed to the Lord than Israel was to her Husband? If He cuts Israel adrift we too will have no assurance about His power to save and keep us.

"As a bridegroom rejoices over his bride, so will your God rejoice over you" (Isaiah 62:5b). What a wonderful day it will be when the whole universe resonates with the sound of the Eternal Lord God rejoicing over those He names as His own. Singing, dancing and rejoicing are part and parcel of a wedding. On some occasions either or both the bride and groom sing. Emotions run high during such a moment. It's impossible to imagine the emotions when the glorious voice of God sings for and over His Bride. (Zephaniah 3:17)

The picture of the Bride is a testimony of the God who loves with an everlasting love. He is faithful to His covenant even though He knows the unfaithfulness of those He has chosen. The Lord of Glory does not close His eyes to the Bride's unwholesome behaviour. He pays the price to rescue her, cleanse her, restore her and beautify her. Why? "Because of the Lord's great love we are not consumed, for his compassions never fail. They are new every morning; great is your faithfulness. I say to myself, 'The Lord is my portion; therefore I will wait for him'" (Lamentations 3:22-24).

Reflect: Does the wedding ceremony take on newer, deeper dimensions when couples who love the Lord become husband and wife? Why?

Prayer: Faithful God, I am resting in your faithfulness and mercy. You know my heart is for you and yet I fail you so often. How grateful I am you will not abandon me to myself. Amen.

Day 30

The Bridegroom

Reading: Matthew 25:1-13

Wedding customs around the globe have their own special elements to emphasize the great occasion. Within the gospels we are faced with the Jewish culture at the time Jesus walked the land of Israel. In statement, parable and involvement Jesus pictures His role as the promised Bridegroom who is to return for His Bride.

Marriages were arranged. The friend of the bridegroom was involved in this process. The man who was the voice crying in the wilderness (John the Baptizer) was given this role. "I am not the Christ but am sent ahead of him. The bride belongs to the bridegroom. The friend who attends the bridegroom waits and listens for him and is full of joy when he hears the bridegroom's voice" (John 3:28-29).

The parables unveil the cultural role of betrothal in preparation for the wedding Day The woman is expected to be ready whilst waiting for the return of the man who will be her husband. The guests must also be ever alert to respond to the call, "He is coming." What is the prospective husband doing between the betrothal and the wedding day? Preparing the place they will call home. This is what Jesus wanted His disciples to understand in John 14:2-3: "In my Father's house are many rooms; if it were not so, I would have told you. I am going there to prepare a place for you. And if I go and prepare a place for you, I will come back and take you to be with me that you may be where I am."

Jesus came to present Himself as the Bridegroom to the Nation of Israel. Across the centuries the way had been prepared through the prophets and the Jewish scriptures for the people to recognize the promised One. The people had become so wayward only a few saw Jesus for who He was. This did not deter Him. Love never gives up. There was, however, a price to pay. The reason is outlined in the prophets. Isaiah chapter one details the nations unwholesome appearance. As the old saying puts it, "Beauty is in the eye of the beholder." To the World, Israel was no longer attractive. God saw things differently. The Lord came to bring life to the spiritually dead, cleansing to the defiled and restoration to the place from which the nation had fallen. The wage for such sin was Death. The Bridegroom was prepared to be the substitute so the one He loved could live again. Was this a waste of love? Is it the greatest example of love ever displayed? So much is wrapped up in the experience of Christ on the Cross but supreme amongst them is Love for the unlovely. This includes everyone who has ever lived. We do not have a tombstone to mark Love's testimony. We have an empty tomb! The victory cry of Love on Easter Sunday is, 'He is risen!'

Before the Lord returned to the Father He commissioned His disciples to be Friends of the Bridegroom. They were to prepare the Bride for her betrothed One's return. Included also in this was an invitation to others to fill the guest list. In the words of Paul to the Corinthians, "I am jealous for you with a godly jealousy. I promised you to one husband, to Christ, so that I might present you as a pure virgin to him" (2 Corinthians 11:2). A miracle is woven in those words. How can anyone be pure in the sight of the Lord who sees the heart? Here is the wonder of grace and the power of Christ's substitution on the cross. The wicked will not inherit the kingdom of God, so we would all miss out. However, "You were washed, you were sanctified, you were justified in the name of the Lord Jesus Christ and by the Spirit of our God" (1 Corinthians 6:11).

The Gospels give us insights into the wonder of the time when the eternal Lord returns to claim His Bride. Combined with the joy of the faithful will be the sorrow of those who didn't believe the person of the Bridegroom and His promise to return. The prophets are the ones who give us insights into the Bridegroom's pleasure as He comes for His betrothed. "In that day, declares the Lord, you will call me my husband…I will betroth you to me for ever; I will betroth you in righteousness and justice, in love and compassion. I will betroth you in faithfulness and you will acknowledge the Lord" (Hosea 2:16, 19). (Read also Psalm 45.)

Reflect: How well am I fulfilling my commission to be a Friend of the Bridegroom?

Prayer: Your word says such a lot about your return, Lord Jesus. It seems such a long time ago you promised to come back and mockers abound. I believe you are faithful; your Word is true, so I ask your grace to keep me looking up. Amen.

Day 31
The Marriage Supper

Reading: Revelation 19:1-9

God loves a party. He is planning a magnificent one to which He invites men and women. What a celebration it will be on two accounts. It will be a victory celebration when the forces of evil will have been overthrown. This allows the Father to rejoice in fulfilling the promise of a wedding to His Son, Jesus Christ. Whilst evil was rampant and not finally judged the marriage between 'the Lamb' and His bride could not take place. In Revelation is the account of dealing with the forces of evil, climaxing in their destruction. After that comes the longed for marriage supper!

The parable of the Wedding Banquet in Matthew 22 holds severe warnings as well as a gracious invitation. The Lord, in this parable, was pointing to the great day of Revelation 19. It is stated the king prepared a wedding banquet for his son and sent out invitations. The ones invited treated it with disrespect and insult. This could not go unchecked. The king punished those who had slandered his son by their words and actions. He therefore widened the guest list to include the poor, the outcast and the disenfranchised. Going to the wedding supper required a certain dress standard. How could such people who responded afford such formal wear? Impossible! Someone must supply it. Grace is beautiful as it gives to the unworthy what is needed yet unaffordable. "Come, all you who are thirsty, come to the waters; and you who have no money, come buy and eat! Come, buy wine and milk without money and without cost....Listen, listen to me, and eat what is good, and your soul will delight in the richest of fare" (Isaiah 55:1-2). Faith is required by the one invited to accept the offer. Knowledge of the one making the offer motivates the faith.

In the parable the king comes across someone who has tried to sneak in on his own terms. How was the king able to recognize this intruder? The man had not accepted the formal wear offered. Did he believe what he was already dressed in should be good enough? Inappropriate dress caused his banishment from the banquet. The requirement for participation in the Heavenly Wedding Supper has been set out. Disregard it at your own risk.

In Revelation 19:8 the required garment is called fine linen, bright and clean. Such a garment stands for the righteous acts of the people of God.

This raises a question. How is it possible for men and women to be righteous? As with the wedding garment in the parable, it must be supplied by the Lord who invites us to the party. Within the New Testament are wonderful invitations to leave the unrighteousness of our human nature at the cross. Bowing before the Lord we gratefully accept, by faith in His promise, His offer of righteousness tried, tested and triumphant. The designer label says, "Made in Heaven, tested in life and death, gifted by Jesus Christ, Lord and Saviour." What we wear in our character, in our actions and in our relationships reflects the One whose label we display. In 1 Corinthians 1:30 we are reminded of this fact. We cannot boast about our goodness, rather our boasting centres upon Christ Jesus. He is our wisdom, our righteousness, our holiness and redemption. Psalm 11:7 tells us the result: "For the Lord is righteous, he loves justice; upright men will see his face."

Where will the festival of grace, the celebration of the wedding supper take place? The passage doesn't say. We need to look into Isaiah 25 for a clue. "On this mountain the Lord Almighty will prepare a feast of rich food for all peoples, a banquet of aged wines – the best of meats and the finest of wines…The Sovereign Lord will wipe away the tears from all faces; he will remove the disgrace of his people from all the earth. The Lord has spoken" (Isaiah 25: 6-8).

What a great day that will be! How gracious is the Heavenly Father in giving us an invitation to be part of this event. Not only an invitation but everything required to stand in His presence and not be embarrassed or dismissed

Reflect: If the Lord called me into His presence now, what garment would I be wearing?

Prayer: Thank you for cleansing me from all that was offensive to you. I am so grateful for the poured out life of my Saviour, which washed me whiter than snow in your sight Heavenly Father. In gratitude I acknowledge you have clothed my nakedness with the righteousness of Jesus my risen Lord. May I wear it with honour. Amen.

I'd Rather...

I'd rather hold your hand in the dark
Than,
Walk in the sunshine with another.

I'd rather grow old with you in marriage
Than,
Enjoy youthful singleness without you.

I'd rather be poor knowing your love
Than,
Financially rich but never meeting you.

Why?
Because
I cannot live without a heart.
You are my heart.

I'd rather share your everyday sorrows
Than,
Laugh with a frivolous company.

I'd rather be a nobody in this world
Than,
A famous celebrity unloved by you.

I'd rather die being your husband
Than,
Live as a king without your embrace.

Why?
Because I cannot deny God's gift!
You are that gift.

Raymond N. Hawkins

www.ingramcontent.com/pod-product-compliance
Lightning Source LLC
Chambersburg PA
CBHW071029080526
44587CB00015B/2553